THE
ULTRALIGHT
STARTUP

THE
ULTRALIGHT
STARTUP

Launching a Business Without Clout or Capital

Jason L. Baptiste

PORTFOLIO / PENGUIN

PORTFOLIO / PENGUIN
Published by the Penguin Group
Penguin Group (USA) Inc., 375 Hudson Street,
New York, New York 10014, U.S.A.
Penguin Group (Canada), 90 Eglinton Avenue East, Suite 700, Toronto,
Ontario, Canada M4P 2Y3 (a division of Pearson Penguin Canada Inc.)
Penguin Books Ltd, 80 Strand, London WC2R 0RL, England
Penguin Ireland, 25 St. Stephen's Green, Dublin 2, Ireland
(a division of Penguin Books Ltd)
Penguin Books Australia Ltd, 250 Camberwell Road, Camberwell,
Victoria 3124, Australia (a division of Pearson Australia Group Pty Ltd)
Penguin Books India Pvt Ltd, 11 Community Centre, Panchsheel Park,
New Delhi – 110 017, India
Penguin Group (NZ), 67 Apollo Drive, Rosedale, Auckland 0632,
New Zealand (a division of Pearson New Zealand Ltd)
Penguin Books (South Africa) (Pty) Ltd, 24 Sturdee Avenue,
Rosebank, Johannesburg 2196, South Africa

Penguin Books Ltd, Registered Offices:
80 Strand, London WC2R 0RL, England

First published in 2012 by Portfolio / Penguin,
a member of Penguin Group (USA) Inc.

10 9 8 7 6 5 4 3 2 1

Library of Congress Cataloging-in-Publication Data

Baptiste, Jason L.
    The ultralight startup : launching a business without clout or capital / Jason
L. Baptiste.
        p. cm.
    Includes index.
    ISBN 978-1-59184-486-0
    1. New business enterprises. 2. New business enterprises—Finance. 3. Entre-
preneurship. I. Title.
    HD62.5.B363 2012
    658.1'1—dc23   2012000615

Printed in the United States of America
Set in ITC New Baskerville Std
Designed by Pauline Neuwirth

Thank you to my mom, dad,
and coworkers at Onswipe for believing

CONTENTS

CONTENTS

THE
ULTRALIGHT
STARTUP

THE BOOK I WISH I HAD HAD WHEN I BECAME AN ENTREPRENEUR

WRITING THIS BOOK has been like starting my business. When my cofounder, Andres Barreto, and I launched our current company, Onswipe, we did so because we saw a need in the marketplace, a need for something we both wish existed (but more on that later). We saw a problem that needed fixing, so we decided to fix it.

For the same reasons, I decided to write this book.

Right now, entrepreneurship is leading the twenty-first-century renaissance, changing the world and the way we think about work. In the past, "entrepreneur" was, at best, a name given to rogue risk takers who couldn't accept authority and, at worst, a code word for those who were either broke and unemployed or rich and bored. Today that is no longer the case. As information and technology have spread, anyone can start a business; and in the postrecession world, in which more of us realize we can't depend on established corporations to keep us employed, entrepreneurship has become not only a respected career path but a necessary one.

The good news is that the barriers to becoming an entrepreneur are lower than ever before and, if you do it right, entrepreneurship can offer fantastic rewards. The Internet has made it possible for anyone to connect with influencers, experts, and potential customers around the world. Moreover, since new companies can exist entirely in the digital space, the costs of launching have reached unprecedented lows.

The bad news is that this trend is so new that there remain very few resources for would-be entrepreneurs, especially in the technology sector, on how to actually start a business. That is why I have written this book. When I was starting out, I had to learn a lot of things by trial and error—how to test an idea, how to market a business, how to raise capital—and I know I could have saved myself (and my cofounder) a lot of grief if someone had given me advice on what to do. This is the book I wish I had had when I got started as a naive and passionate entrepreneur at the tender age of nineteen. I hope it will help and inspire you to pursue your passion while avoiding some of the mistakes I made.

EVERYTHING YOUR MBA BROTHER TOLD YOU IS WRONG

It seems as if everyone has a brother, cousin, sister, uncle, parent, or next-door neighbor with an MBA who thinks starting a successful company just isn't possible. That's because MBAs have been trained to look at business from a much more formal and complicated perspective than you do. When they think of entrepreneurship, they think of the traditional meaning—the one that requires a business plan, long-term financial projections, a ton of up-front capital, and an Ivy League degree just to launch a business, let alone to make it succeed. But luckily as times have changed, so have the rules.

Plus, MBAs are designed for those who want to be executives or managers at large Fortune 500 companies. But running a startup presents a completely different set of challenges, and having outside formalized training may harm your ability to move as fast as possible. So stop listening to the MBAs and any other naysayers. It's time to free your mind.

WHO THIS BOOK IS FOR

The goal of this book is to provide a simple and straightforward blueprint for creating a startup from scratch—with little up-front capital, little experience, or few connections in your industry. You will learn how to come up with an idea, build a simple first version of the product, and gain customers, then take it to the next level with fund-raising. You'll notice that although many of the principles laid out here can be applied to a lot of industries, most of them are specifically targeted to the technology sector. I did this for two reasons: 1) My experience is in this space, so I can speak about it as an expert, someone who has been there; and 2) technology is a much more accessible industry to enter than many others because it requires less capital than more traditional businesses. If you want to become the next Facebook or Twitter or Dropbox, this book is for you. You might feel very far away from reaching your goals right now, but remember, even today's most successful companies started as nothing more than a group of individuals with an idea.

WHAT THIS BOOK WILL DO

This book will teach a very specific set of skills an entrepreneur needs. By the time you finish reading it you should be able to do the following things:

1. Fully formulate an idea for your startup.
2. Find cofounders and talent.
3. Release an idea into the wild in a weekend.
4. Get press.
5. Get customers from Day One.
6. Raise money.

A quick note: This is a relatively short book, but it contains a primer on all the important steps you'll need to take when building your startup, and should be enough to get you started. But if you want more information, there are tons of other resources out there about how to start a company, work the press, and find talent.

WHY SHOULD YOU LISTEN TO ME?

I know that all the advice in this book will help you because I've used it myself. I started my first company at nineteen (it failed) and my second company, Cloudomatic, in 2010, when I was twenty-three. Currently I'm the cofounder and CEO of Onswipe, a startup that works with publishers to format Web site content on tablet platforms. The principles here are the same ones that helped us build our modest two-person startup into a legit business worth tens of millions of dollars. This book is not about me, though. It is about what I learned along the way. I will use stories from my experiences (as well as those of other entrepreneurs) to illustrate the ideas and advice in the book. But ultimately I want this book to be about *you*.

A FEW WORDS ON DROPPING OUT OF COLLEGE

I was still in college when I started my first business, and some of the biggest companies (take Facebook) were born on campuses. My guess is that some of you are currently in school and toying with the idea of dropping out to pursue your dream. But before you do, you should think twice. It's true, you won't learn the skills it takes to be an entrepreneur by sitting in a classroom, but before you quit, you should consider your circumstances fully.

In 2007, when I was a junior in college, I dropped out of school to work on a startup I'd been building for a year. When the company failed eighteen months later, I returned to school to finish my degree instead of launching another company. I did this because I needed a breather while I got myself organized, and also because I wanted to finish what I had started—a goal that's important for every entrepreneur.

I don't regret dropping out. I learned a lot of things while I was out of school and I had a blast doing it. However, I had been careful. I didn't leave school until my idea was gaining traction and I had my finances in order. If I had been able to dedicate to my company the time it required while staying in school, I would have. But I became so busy that I had to choose. The point is, I didn't quit until I had something to quit for. Before you drop out, consider whether it's really necessary.

BEFORE WE BEGIN

The subtitle of this book promises to show you how to create a company without a lot of money. But that does not mean that starting a company is cheap or easy. There's no magic bullet that will make starting one cost nothing, and there's no way to start a company without putting in a lot of work.

The goal of this book is to help entrepreneurs avoid the silly mistakes I made when I started and reduce the friction-filled learning curve. There's no way to avoid the difficulties of entrepreneurship, but there are certainly ways to make the process smoother. Just the way a great product reduces friction between a user and what they want, this book is meant to reduce friction between an entrepreneur and the tasks he should be working on.

Of course, you should not take my words as gospel or fail to seek advice elsewhere. I can tell you only what has worked for me and what has worked for the people around me, but every situation is different. I hope you will find your own style and have fun doing it. My goal is not to prove myself right. It is to inspire and help you so you can one day enjoy the freedom and opportunities that entrepreneurship brings.

1

IT ALL STARTS WITH AN IDEA

EVERY GREAT BUSINESS starts with a great idea. Maybe you already have an idea you're working on. Maybe you have one but you're not sure if it's any good. Or maybe you just like the idea of starting something of your own but aren't sure what that should be yet. Regardless of where you are, this chapter should help you brainstorm or sharpen an idea.

HOW JOBS AND WOZNIAK GOT THE IDEA FOR APPLE

Large companies often have red tape and bureaucracy that make it take way too long for anything to happen. If you have ever tried to get a cool project started or get the IT department to take care of something, odds are you will likely age a few years before it ever gets done. Some of the best startups are born from recognizing the problems that exist at your current employer, but which will never see the light of day. Take advantage of these gaps.

One of these gaps is how Apple got started. At the time of Apple's founding, Steve "Woz" Wozniak wanted to create a better computer that would be suited for personal home use. This was monumental because, at the time, computers were only for professional use, not personal home use. Wozniak discovered the problem—the absence of a personal computer—and decided to solve it. When Woz checked with Hewlett-Packard, his employer at the time, to see whether he could continue with the project or whether HP wanted the rights to what would become Apple Computer, his boss said, "No one will ever want a personal computer." With HP not interested in pursuing the project or having the rights to it, Woz and Jobs were free and clear to build what would become Apple.

FIND A PROBLEM
THAT NEEDS TO BE SOLVED

If you are stumped about what you should build or feel that you don't have the perfect idea, don't worry. There is no perfect idea, but there are tons of problems that need to be solved.

This is how Onswipe came to be. My cofounder, Andres, and I had started blogging as a side project, but when we tried to view our sites on our iPads, the content looked terrible. We wondered if there was some way to build a service that would help publishers like us make their sites look great without dealing with annoying application developers and vendors. Eureka! We had an idea.

What made this idea so great, though, was that not only

would it solve our problem, it would solve a lot of other people's problems as well. There was an automatic, built-in audience of people who would be looking for the same solution we were.

When looking for inspiration, start with yourself. Ask yourself what service or product you wish existed. What would make your life easier? What would you be willing to pay for? Starting with yourself is not only the easiest way to come up with a great idea, it's also an easy way to keep yourself motivated because you know that even if you don't become a billionaire on your first try, you'll at least have built something that you can use to make your life easier.

Here are a few other things to keep in mind when trying to find a problem to solve.

It Doesn't Have to Be Sexy to Make Money

There is a ton of money to be made in unsexy industries that often get little press or no attention. The key to winning in an unsexy industry is to develop a simple and great product that delights a user. Competition among sexy companies (like today's social media and daily deals sites) is fierce, but incumbents in less popular areas often grow comfortable and stick with the status quo rather than try to innovate. Since they're often the only player, they don't need to do much to win. But just because customers flock to these companies doesn't mean they're satisfied with what they're getting. If you can figure out a way to improve upon an old, established model, you can make a lot of people happy while making a lot of money.

One example of this is Square, which was started by Jack Dorsey, the cofounder and inventor of Twitter. After creating one of the world's sexiest and fastest growing services, Jack could easily have gone after the next big thing and done it all over again. Instead he went after an unsexy and unchanged industry: real-life merchant processing. Jack set out to make it easy for merchants of all sizes to accept credit card payments on mobile devices such as the iPad and iPhone. Before Square, merchants had to go through a long, drawn-out approval process, and that's only if they were lucky enough to be eligible. The approval process existed, not out of pure necessity, but as a lack of innovation to move fast to get merchants active with a payment processor. Square eliminates the approval process yet prevents fraud. Using a simple, easy to use, and elegant interface without charging extraneous transaction or equipment fees, Square now processes over one million dollars of payments a day while shaking up existing multibillion-dollar incumbents such as VeriFone, which has been around for decades.

You Don't Have to Be New, You Just Have to Be Better

The world is short on truly original ideas. Pretty much everything has been tried before in some way. But just because someone currently has the best solution on the market doesn't mean the case is closed. Even accepted models have room for improvement, and sometimes all it takes to be the hot new thing is finding a way to do an old thing better. Take a look at Dropbox, a service I have used for many years and think every entrepreneur should use. Before Dropbox existed, the online storage market had been saturated by competitors, leaving what many thought was little room for newcomers. Microsoft alone had five storage products! So when Drew Houston created Dropbox, no one thought he could do better and many thought he was wasting his time. Not only was there a lot of competition, but there were low margins and high customer acquisition costs as well.

But Dropbox overcame these obstacles and is now the world's leading online storage provider worth hundreds of millions of dollars. Even though there were many other services in the space, they were all difficult to use or didn't function smoothly. Dropbox's service was better than all the others' because of its simplicity and the fact that it just worked better then they did. Their great product also allowed Dropbox to overcome the difficulty of high customer acquisition costs because when new customers realized how great it was, they spread the word.

Do Something That Used to Be Impossible

The best products take advantage of new technologies that can be applied to an idea to make a truly innovative product. Onswipe is a prime example of this. We not only focused on building a product that didn't exist, but we used a new technology (HTML5) to do it. This gave us an even bigger edge because while other people were still fiddling with old technologies, we were mastering something new. Use the following suggestions as building blocks for your idea to make sure that you are headed where the ball is going, not where it's already landed.

Stay Connected

Judging from trends in the past few years, it's pretty safe to assume that sometime in the very near future all electronic devices will be connected to the Internet. Sure, we have had the Internet for a couple of decades now, but until quite recently you could only access it from certain places and devices. What will it mean when any technology you build can always be connected anywhere in the world? In today's world of mobile devices, you should build something that takes advantage of the ability always to be connected to high-speed Internet.

Be Location Aware

Companies like Foursquare have taken advantage of geolocational software that allows them to pinpoint where users are at any given moment. If most devices are untethered, then what can you do if you can access the location of a user? More purchases happen in the real world and locally than online, which presents a world of new business models. Build something that can take advantage not only of the local surroundings, but also of the actual people nearby. If all applications are socially connected, then how can you use location to make your product work even better?

Make It Touch Enabled

I'm biased, but I also have deep domain expertise in understanding why touch interfaces will soon outpace point-and-click interfaces. In the past, the user experience was limited to what could be accomplished with a mouse and keyboard, but that is quickly changing. When we first started Onswipe, the estimate for when touch devices (including tablets and touch-enabled smartphones like the iPhone) would outpace traditional point-and-click devices was for the third quarter of 2012, but it was quickly revised to the very end of the fourth quarter of 2011. Touch is important because it allows companies to build a more personal, interactive experience for their users, and this is a huge selling point. And users seem to prefer it. In what ways can you integrate touch into your product to help connect with users?

Get Social

Five years ago it was really difficult to build consumer Web products because you needed to have a large user base before you could do anything of interest. Now, thanks to services like Facebook Connect and Twitter, you can tap into your existing users' network of friends. The types of applications you can build will now benefit from having access to the viral distribution of more than eight hundred million people. At Onswipe we allow readers to see what their friends are reading across all the different publications we power. This would be much more difficult to accomplish if not for Facebook Connect and Twitter.

Break It Down

Before iTunes came along, music companies thought they could only make money by selling whole albums, not individual songs. But Apple realized that by making the transaction digital, instantaneous, and cheap, companies could get a lot of people to buy music—even those who would not have shelled out fifteen dollars for a CD. Now there are tons of things you can buy for this price—books, magazines, and apps among them. Google is also good at this. By charging per click instead of making companies buy huge packages, they're able to extract a large quantity of small transactions from advertisers. Rather than figuring out how to extract a lot of money from people at once, figure out how to extract a little bit over a long period of time.

Be Compatible

We live in a world in which almost everyone has several devices—computers, phones, tablets, Internet-connected TVs, gaming consoles, e-readers, car navigation systems—that can all be synced. When developing your product, don't just focus on how it will work with one device, even if it's specifically designed for it. Figure out how you can sync it with others.

Amazon does a great job of this with their Kindle service. You can download and pay for a book, then read it on your iPad, continue where you left off on your iPhone, then finish the book on your Kindle device. Until someone comes up with a device that does everything (and is portable), users are going to demand compatibility.

LOOK AT YOUR IDEA UNDER A MICROSCOPE

Once you have come up with a great idea, take a moment to play devil's advocate with yourself. It's much better to come to terms now with any roadblocks or problems your idea presents rather than see it collapse later on. At worst, you may have to go back to the drawing board, but most likely this process will help you figure out how to make the idea more feasible. You don't need to seek validation and feedback from outsiders just yet (we'll get to that later), but you might also want to turn to a few trusted advisers, as they will be less biased than you. To get started, ask yourself the following questions.

How Will You Make Your First Dollar?

Most entrepreneurs fall into one of two opposite categories: those who think about how they will make money or those who don't. Your idea may be so awesome that it's easy to imagine making your first million, but when evaluating a potential startup idea, you need to think about how you will make your first dollar. Another way to phrase this question is: *When* will you make this first dollar? If the answer is some time far in the future, odds are that you will go out of business before you make a cent.

Onswipe started as a simple WordPress plugin for which we charged fifty dollars. We charged for the plugin because we knew that it is hard to get people to pay for something from a brand-new startup. People are cheap, and convincing them that you provide value takes a lot of work. When you're starting out, the difference between zero dollars and any number greater than zero dollars is huge. By partnering with WordPress, we were able to get hundreds of people to pay us. That's when we knew we were on to something of tremendous value. We never intended to stick with the plugin idea, but it served as a litmus test to determine just how much value there was in the concept. After that, we knew we could make money.

Do You Have Domain Expertise?

Hopeful entrepreneurs often go into fields they have zero expertise in, but if you do this you will spend a lot of time trying to gain the knowledge necessary to be successful. Knowledge can come through personal passion for the space or years of work in it. It's a huge leg up to have it beforehand and will help you avoid amateur mistakes. It's much easier to work with what you know than to learn something new.

If you don't have all the expertise you need, find people you can work with—whether they be employees, investors, or advisers—who do.

An example of a company that does this well is the group payments platform WePay. Payments is one of the toughest and most grueling areas in which to create a startup because it requires a ton of deep domain expertise in security and fraud detection. Knowing this, WePay founders Bill Clerico and Rich Aberman reached out to an investor named Max Levchin. Max was the cofounder and CTO of PayPal, where his job was dealing with fraud, cryptography, and payment processing. By landing Max as an investor, WePay was able to build credibility by avoiding obvious mistakes.

Are You Really Passionate About This Idea?

Every idea gets an entrepreneur excited for the first twenty-four hours. But the true test is whether you are still passionate about your idea months after you come up with it. No idea will make you a millionaire overnight. It's a long, hard road until your startup is successful, and if you lose the passion to keep going you are sure to stall out. Stop thinking about the idea right now for one week and then come back to it. Are you still excited by it? That's the ultimate test of whether the idea will give you the same stomach butterflies years down the road.

How Big Is the Market?

People often fall in love with ideas that just can't be turned into sustainable companies. If you want your startup to grow, you need to go after a large market. If you hope to receive venture funding, know that venture capital firms look for companies that have the potential to do great things in enormous markets. It's possible you have a great idea, but if the market for it is too small, it's better to turn it into a side project.

On the flip side, if the market you're thinking of entering is small but there's no other competition, you might have an opportunity to be a big fish in a small pond.

How Crowded Is the Market?

As I mentioned earlier, it's hard to enter a crowded market, but it's completely possible when the incumbent has a bad product. There are two types of crowded markets:

1. Established crowded markets in which an incumbent exists but refuses to do anything innovative.

2. Hot crowded markets with many fast-moving, innovative players trying to take a piece of the pie. In these markets, clear leaders usually emerge fast, leaving every-

one else to settle for scraps. It's innovation's version of Russian roulette.

You should avoid hot crowded markets. Sure, you can win big in them, but it's a gamble and you're more likely to succeed elsewhere. As I write this the group chat space is a perfect example of a hot crowded market. Many companies have entered the space even though only a few have gotten attention. GroupMe has succeeded by selling for eighty-five million dollars, but many others have failed to gain traction.

How Simple Will It Be to Ship a First Version of the Product?

Some ideas are really complicated and require a ton of capital and a long time before a first version can be released. Since this book is for those who don't have a ton of capital, you should go after an idea that will allow you to ship (that is, release) a first version as quickly as possible. If it will take too long, try to find a simpler form of the idea that you can build on. Ask yourself, "What is the most basic version I can build to get started in the next sixty days?" Keep in mind that Facebook started out at one school and allowed users to post only one photo when it launched in 2004.

Start a Project, Not a Company

It's good to keep the big picture in mind and to have long-term goals in the beginning, but you've got to start small. Don't get caught up in the grand vision. Instead, think of yourself as working on a project, not a company. The difference here is that if you're working on a project, you can focus on creating something cool without the pressure for long-term success. Companies, on the other hand, have to focus on growing and making money because many other individuals, like coworkers, investors, and customers, depend upon them.

If you're still in school, this difference is even more beneficial because the worst-case scenario is that your project goes nowhere but you learn something along the way. Spare yourself the stress of a startup and use your time in college to experiment.

HOW FOURSQUARE GOT STARTED

Even though Foursquare has become very popular very quickly, the idea began many, many years ago—long before it turned into what it is today.

Foursquare's origins can be traced all the way back to 2001 when CEO and cofounder Dennis Crowley was laid off, along with a large number of his colleagues, from a hot New York City startup called Vindigo. All of a sudden, a bunch of people who were used to spending every day and night with each other were dispersed to separate lives collecting unemployment checks. Unable to keep up with what everyone was doing, Dennis created a simple app that let people state where they were. The app, which Dennis named Dodgeball, gained traction but never really took off.

A few years later, in 2004, Dennis joined New York University's Interactive Telecommunications Program (ITP). As part of the program, he had to do a research project involving technology, so Dennis decided to revive Dodgeball and give it another go. It started taking off in the New York City area, attracting a fair number of users and interest from investors. Along the way, Dennis met some of the folks from Google, who thought what he was up to was pretty neat. They offered to buy Dodgeball and bring Dennis and his cofounder, Alex Rainert, into Google. Now Dodgeball was a part of Google.

But Google neglected Dodgeball as a product, never giving it the attention and resources it needed to take off. This frustrated Dennis and Alex, so in 2007 they decided to quit Google and return to the world of startups. Dodgeball stayed alive for a couple more years until Google scheduled to shut it down in early 2009.

Dennis had moved on from working with other startups and wanted to take a shot at his location-based network concept again. By now the iPhone and Android phones had taken hold in the marketplace and the time seemed ripe to take advantage of this mobile technology. Foursquare launched at South by Southwest in 2009 and was a complete hit. From there it's grown to millions of users and is worth hundreds of millions of dollars.

Looking at the almost decadelong saga of Foursquare, three lessons jump out:

1. **The founders built something they wanted.** The original idea for Foursquare took hold because Dennis and Alex needed a way to stay connected to their former colleagues. They started a project to create something they wanted for themselves.

2. **They were passionate about the idea.** Dennis and Alex kept working at something they wanted to see exist. The

idea wouldn't go away, and they kept going until, after years of trial and error, their hard work finally paid off.

3. **They waited for the technology to be more mature.** In order for Foursquare to make sense, Dennis and Alex had to wait for the mobile technology of smartphones to take hold in the market. Once that happened, they jumped at the chance to take advantage of it.

2

HOW TO LAUNCH FASTER THAN YOU EVER IMAGINED

NOW THAT YOU have your idea picked out, you'll want to start bringing it to market. You could easily spend millions trying to perfect your product before you get it out the door, but thanks to something called the minimum viable product you don't have to and, in fact, you shouldn't.

Popularized by entrepreneur and tech blogger Eric Ries, the minimum viable product is the simplest form of a product you can build in order to gain interest. It's basically a Web site that includes screenshots of the product you're building. In most cases it is not a working version of the product, but a prototype to help you harvest and evaluate interest among potential users.

There are two types of MVPs: minimal feature set MVPs and smoke test MVPs. The minimal features set requires that you build a working product, but the smoke test simply showcases a few elements of the product you hope to build. The smoke test is much quicker and cheaper to produce since it requires less technical knowledge, so we're going to focus on that type of MVP.

Smoke test MVPs shouldn't cost a lot of money, especially if you have technical and design knowledge and can do most of the work on your own. If you have to hire a designer you'll end up spending more, but realistically you can expect to pay one hundred dollars to two hundred dollars.

Here are five characteristics that every MVP should include:

1. **A crystal clear message of the product's value proposition.** In order to get the right feedback and make sure your idea is being evaluated properly, you have to clearly and accurately explain what your product is. In the MVP stage, the message is far more important than the design of the product itself. You can have a great looking MVP, but if people don't know what it is or how it can help them, it's nothing more than artwork.

2. **A design and interface that resembles the finished product.** Try to make potential users believe they are looking at a finished product. Yes, the design might not be perfect, but potential users need to interact with your product in a way that will make them want to pay for it later.

3. **A way to get feedback.** The whole point of an MVP is to get feedback before you launch the final version into the whole market. There are a lot of ways to do this, which I'll discuss later in the book.

4. **A clear and short road to release.** An MVP should take a maximum of two weeks to put together. The more time you spend on an MVP, the more unnecessary things you start to add and the easier it is to lose focus on the three important points just listed.

5. **A groundwork on which to build the product.** If the MVP is a success and you decide to move forward, you already will have done a large amount of work. When building the MVP, think of each element as something you may be able to use later on.

THE GENESIS OF CLOUDOMATIC

Before Andres and I started Onswipe, we founded a company called Cloudomatic, which was later acquired. Throughout this chapter, I will use the story of Cloudomatic to illustrate how to build an MVP. I hope you will learn from our successes—and failures.

The first version of Cloudomatic was launched as a directory of Web-based software for businesses. We later recognized the need to provide the transaction and referral engine for Software as a Service (SaaS) businesses so we developed a second product known as Cloudomatic(flow). We knew we had a good idea, but we wanted to test it out before we built the finished product, so Andres and I locked ourselves away for a weekend to get something ready for Monday morning.

To make things easier on ourselves, we used WordPress to create our smoke test MVP. Most people think of WordPress as a blogging platform, but it's also used by many companies to power their official Web sites. WordPress allowed us to get up and running with everything we needed almost immediately rather than having to create the site from scratch.

STEP 1: CRAFT YOUR HYPOTHESIS

An MVP is a type of experiment on your product and, as with a regular science experiment, you should have a hypothesis to test as you move forward. Make an educated guess about what you expect will happen so that you have something to pay attention to in the experiment. Some elements you should include in your hypothesis are:

- **Do people want your product?** It's possible that people have already shown demand for your product, but in most cases this is what you're trying to gauge with an MVP. One of the major benefits of an MVP is learning whether a potential user will want your product before you spend months building it.

- **Will people pay for your product?** Pricing is one of the most difficult aspects of building a startup. If you think people will be willing to pay a certain amount, you can test that with your MVP, as well as what metrics they will base their price sensitivity upon. We'll take a look at how you should price your product later on.

- **Will people want a particular feature more than others?** Everyone is different and will want your product to include different features. If you listened to all your potential users' demands you would constantly be building something new, most likely at the expense of your core service. With an MVP, you can get a large dataset of feature requests and then prioritize which ones to focus on based upon overall demand.

- **Will people perceive the product in a certain way?** Perception is one of the least talked about concepts when it comes to startups. You may have a specific vision of what your product is and why it's useful, but that doesn't mean your users will see things the same way. An MVP is a great way for you to clarify how the world views your product and, if necessary, take the steps to change it.

How Cloudomatic Did It

As software entrepreneurs, Andres and I knew how difficult it was for companies to find Web-based software to help them run their businesses. We knew there was a market for a service that would help them find these resources, but we didn't know how big the market was. With our MVP we set out with one main hypothesis and two smaller ones:

Main hypothesis. Web-based software developers do not have the time or resources to build a referral program, but desperately want one as a proper customer acquisition channel.

Small hypothesis 1. Developers will be willing to share a cut of revenue from a transaction instead of paying a monthly fee so that the business model allows the revenue generated to grow proportionately to the number of people using the product.

Small hypothesis 2. Users will understand the difference between a traditional affiliate program, which helps companies get more customers by letting existing customers refer new ones, and what we're offering, which is more of a partner and referral program. Partner and referral programs are about leveraging individuals who are already users familiar with your product.

STEP 2: OUTLINE YOUR SPECIFICATIONS

Before you design your MVP, you need to create detailed specifications for what is being built. These will become the blueprint for your future product and will guide you later on as you continue to develop it. In the case of your MVP, this step is very important because it gives you an overall picture of the product and allows you to see what elements need to be showcased in the MVP. Here's how you should create a feature specification:

- **Have a stated goal.** At the top of your specifications outline, write down your goal for the product you are building in a few words or sentences. This will set the tone and frame of reference for how the specifications are created and added to. If something does not fall in line with the goal, don't include it.
- **Outline the roles of each type of potential user.** Your product may be used by multiple classes of individuals, all of whom will use it for different things. By defining these roles, you can more easily figure out how to organize your MVP so that each group understands the functionality of your product for its own purposes.
- **Divide individual features of the product into sections.** Each major piece of functionality should be in its

own section so users will clearly understand what each feature accomplishes. Features are things such as letting users set up their branding inside a product, upload a photo, or import their contact lists. Breaking these down will also help you figure out which groups of features you want to showcase in the MVP.

How Cloudomatic Did It

Below is a sample of the actual specifications I created for Cloudomatic(flow) before we built our MVP. I have only included a small sample because the full specifications are way too long and probably wouldn't help you much anyway. This example is intended to be a guide, not something you should copy. Figure out what works for you.

CLOUDOMATIC(FLOW) SPECIFICATION SHEET

Goal: To provide simple and hosted affiliate software for SaaS developers.

Overview of Roles
- Application Developers: The owners of the applications being provided.
- Application Partners: Those promoting the applications.
- Application User: Those who are referred to an application by a partner.

Features Overview

Sign-up Form

- Purpose: Allows a developer to sign up for an account with Cloudomatic(flow)
- Feature Inclusions
- E-mail Address (Developer_E-mail)
  - Example: example@saasapp.com
- Developer Name (Developer_Real_Name)
  - Example: John Doe
- Developer Company Name (Developer_Company_Name)
  - Example: SaaSApp
- Choose Password (Developer_Password)
  - Example: password1234
- Confirm Password:
  - Example: password 1234

The goal is to come up with a well-organized, clear blueprint for what you will be building. You won't know exactly what the final product will look like but you should know what it will do. At this stage, the process is all about function over form.

STEP 3: CREATE WIREFRAMES FOR THE SPECS YOU WANT TO FEATURE

Now that you have specifications outlined, you need to create wireframes. Wireframes are graphical representations that show how each feature should be designed in the final product. You can create wireframes even if you have very little technical knowledge because they are merely guidelines for how you want the final MVP to look. Once you have the wireframes created, you will give them to a designer to build the final screenshots that you will feature on your site. The best way to start building wireframes is to draw inspiration from existing products that have done well. You don't want to rip anyone off, but understanding how a similar company has designed their application or Web site can make life a lot easier. Remember, your goal is to build something decent in a short period of time. There is no need to reinvent the wheel.

Create wireframes for every section of your specification. Only a small portion of the wireframes will need to be turned into actual screenshots for your MVP, but going through the wireframing process will help you realize which screens need to be created.

The spec should be your canon for putting together wireframes. Do not add elements to the page that you did not plan for. If you add elements once, you will most likely do it many times in the future.

At this stage, don't worry about making anything pretty. That's what designers are for. You should also not bother writing copy or having proper data filled in. Once your wireframes have been turned into an actual design, you will fill in the copy.

How Cloudomatic Did It

Below is an example of one of the wireframes we created after we completed our spec sheet. This wireframe shows the breakdown of an application developer's revenue from their partner program.

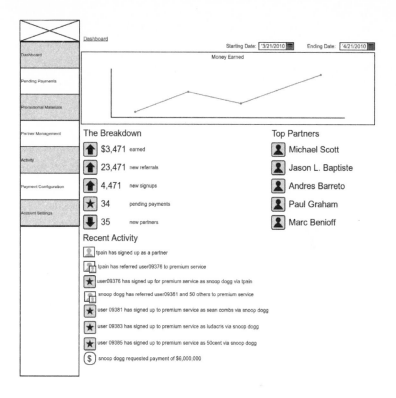

STEP 4: TURN THE WIREFRAMES INTO DESIGNS

A great design won't make up for bad specifications in your MVP, but you do need to create something that will make potential users want to sign up. Now that you've created wireframes for each product specification, you can move to the design stage and really start building your MVP.

Pick 3 wireframes to become actual designs. I'm sure you have at least five to ten wireframes that you would like to turn into actual designs, but there is no reason to. Remember, you're building an MVP, not the final product, and you should focus on the specifications that will really get users' attention. Pick the three wireframes that are the most important and the most different from one another. Later on, when you build the final product, you can use these three designs as templates for all your other wireframes.

Find your designer. I will explore in another chapter how to find the best talent to work with you in your startup, but you need a designer now. If you already have one on your team or are confident in your design skills, feel free to move ahead. If not, try asking friends and colleagues if they know of anyone or check out sites like 99Designs or oDesk to find a freelancer who can complete your project quickly.

Revise and polish. After the design is complete, make sure to perfect the aspects of the design that are really important in selling the product. Remember, your main goal is to generate intent and figure out who would be willing to sign up for the product. Make sure that the designs are polished and well focused on the points you think will let you harvest the most intent possible. The simple way to do this is to find two features in each screenshot that are most important and focus on those.

How Cloudomatic Did It

Andres and I wanted to make sure our three different types of users would understand how our product worked for them. We had one screenshot for software developers and one screenshot for their affiliates and partners. We were lucky enough to have already worked with a great designer, Armando, from our Cloudomatic offering, so we knew we could rely on him this time around as well. Today, Armando is part of the Onswipe team.

After he gave us his designs, we polished the elements we thought were most important. We knew that most developers would be concerned with how the product worked and what type of data they got from us about the businesses we partnered them with. We focused on the screen that let developers customize their programs and the screen that showed the greatest amount of data.

STEP 5: WRITE THE COPY FOR THE SITE

Besides a few screenshots, the only thing you have to communicate your message is the copy you write for the site itself. Every word on a minimum viable product's Web site matters and should not be overlooked. Your MVP site should have four key pages of copy.

Home Page

The home page will often be the first page someone sees and if you don't make a good impression it will also be the last.

That means the copy you put here is the most crucial of any copy on the site. It needs to provide key information about the product while also keeping visitors interested in perusing the site. To do this, you need to include:

ONE-LINE CATCHPHRASE

This is a way for you to describe your product to someone very easily, and if you do it right it will become how you define your product later on. For Onswipe, we use "Insanely Easy Tablet Publishing," four words that our target users understand. The catchphrase should be no longer than seven words.

FOUR SUPPORTING POINTS

These expand on your online catchphrase to offer a little more information about your product's value proposition. With Onswipe, the value proposition was simple: tens of millions of readers can view your Web content from an iPad. We let you provide a more engaging experience and derive more revenues from these visitors.

Screenshots of Your Minimum Viable Product

The screenshots of your minimum viable product should appear on the home page above the fold (the part of your site a user sees as soon as they land on the page and before they scroll down). To save space, you can include thumbnails of each screenshot that blow up when clicked on. Each screenshot should include a one-sentence overview of what is being shown.

A PARAGRAPH TO REDUCE CONFUSION

The one paragraph overview of your service should dig deeper into what the product is about. Ask yourself, "What will people be most confused about?," and let this paragraph focus on reducing confusion. Do not use buzzwords or confusing hyperbole. Get straight to the point, be clear, and be concise.

Features Overview

The features overview will really help to sell those who want to know more about your product. Here are things to keep in mind when describing your features:

FIGURE OUT WHO IS NOT YOUR CUSTOMER

The goal of the MVP is to get feedback from the people who are most likely to become your customers, so don't waste time trying to attract people who are not your customers. Remembering this will let you stay focused and help you figure out which features are most important.

BREAK FEATURES DOWN BY ROLES

Many different people will visit your MVP and they will often check out the features that benefit them. Customers are selfish individuals. They want to know that they will be taken care of and that the product will cater to them. If you break down the features based on who will derive the most benefit from them, potential users will be able to focus on what matters to them.

GIVE PRIORITY TO YOUR SCREENSHOTS

Give priority to the features that are showcased in your screen-shots. You have determined that these features are your most valuable propositions and they have a visual cue to go with them. They should be highlighted front and center to visitors.

FREQUENTLY ASKED QUESTIONS SECTION

A frequently asked questions page allows you to address specific questions people may have. A few things to keep in mind:

Too much is never enough. Answer every question imaginable in the FAQ. If you think even one person will ask a certain question, answer it here. This page is not meant to be short and to the point like the home page.

Dumb questions come first. People are lazy when it comes to finding information. Even if something seems obvious you should include it on your FAQ. Visitors will often skip right to the FAQ rather than poke around your site to figure things out for themselves so make sure the biggest questions are answered first.

Break questions down by section. Your FAQ should have a table of contents-like element at the top that links to different sections. The sections should be broken down into categories that cover specific features, general questions, pricing, privacy, and anything else that you feel warrants its own section.

DON'T IGNORE PRICING

One section that's important to include is pricing. If you know your pricing model—which you probably won't at this stage—you should give details here. If you do not know your pricing model, be transparent and honest. The best middle ground is to give the metrics upon which your pricing will be based (e.g., time, usage, number of subscribers, etc.).

Contact Page

The contact page is very simple but it's an important part of a minimum viable product. Since the product is not launched yet, potential customers will be wary of what you are up to. By opening a clear line of communication you can make potential customers feel reassured. Here are the key lines of communication that you should have open to gain trust:

E-MAIL

This is the way most customers will probably want to communicate with you. Make sure to include an e-mail address associated with the domain you are using for your MVP. Don't use something generic and impersonal like contact@yourdomain.com, but founders@yourdomain.com. Using an e-mail address that reaches the founders adds a level of trust and personality.

TWITTER

Twitter used to be used only by transparent companies that communicated well with the public. Now everyone has to use it and people will wonder if you're not active on it. By having a Twitter account attached to your minimum viable product, it is far more likely that people will look at the product as more trustworthy and not something set up over the course of a weekend.

BONUS: TELEPHONE

This may seem excessive or old-fashioned, but an open telephone line can go a very long way in building a relationship with potential customers. People want to know they can connect with someone one-on-one, not just through a computer screen.

How Cloudomatic Did It

As I said above, the hardest and most crucial copy to write is what goes on your home page, so I'm going to show you how Andres and I did this for Cloudomatic(flow).

Before we started writing the copy itself, we outlined everything we wanted to communicate:

- We were building a product primarily for software developers.
- We were building for recurring revenue models.
- We were building for software that was not downloadable.

- We wanted to charge something but we weren't sure about the exact price.
- We wanted to highlight that this was more about referral and partners than affiliates, which can be scammy.
- We wanted to show that integration would be simple and would work with any software provider.

From there we came up with the simple tagline "Simple Partner Software." This was straightforward but it left a lot to the imagination. So we added four supporting points:

1. **Focused on Web apps.** We were focused on a main set of customers—Web developers who made software for small businesses. These developers deliver software in the Web browser instead of in a download.

2. **Integrated with Cloudomatic.** We knew that our existing customers would want to know how they could take advantage of this new service, so we wanted to communicate that they would be included in the new program.

3. **Pricing that scales.** People want to know they are paying for something of value, so we highlighted the fact that they would only have to pay for the amount of service they got.

4. **Dead simple.** This one is pretty straightforward. People don't like when things are complicated, so we wanted to reassure customers that the product would be easy to use.

Finally, to help reduce any confusion, we added a paragraph that explained what we did. Here's our example:

Cloudomatic(flow) is an easy-to-integrate affiliate and partner engine specifically made for business Web apps/SaaS. Cloudomatic(flow) has no sign-up fees, monthly fees, or minimum transaction amounts. We only make money when you make money.

Now that you've created your MVP, it's time to put it out into the real world.

3

TESTING YOUR PRODUCT IN THE REAL WORLD

YOU CAN BUILD a minimum viable product, but until you test it in the real world with some level of scale, your hypotheses mean absolutely nothing. If you have no clout or capital, getting people to notice your MVP can be extremely difficult. Sure, you can hustle and hustle to convince people to use it, but this is a lot of work with sometimes very little payoff. At this stage it might be best and more efficient for you to spend a little bit of money on a service that will attract potential users to evaluate your MVP. Another advantage of this approach is that rather than relying on feedback from people you know or interact with—who may or may not be honest in their assessment—it gives you the chance to see how the average user will respond to your product in the real world. But before you start spending money, there are a few things you need to consider.

STEP 1: DECIDE HOW TO COLLECT FEEDBACK

Getting feedback is the number one priority of your MVP. However, you should not and probably will not get all the feedback you need at this stage. Right now you are looking to get feedback fast, and you will not have time to collect all the feedback the market can possibly provide. Even though you can probably gather a lot of it in the first weekend after you go live, it could take two to three weeks to sift through all of it. How you decide to collect feedback is ultimately dependent upon two key things:

1. The metrics that define success.
2. Your success and failure scenarios.

The Metrics That Define Success

These are different for every potential product and idea. Some of the metrics can be objective and some can be subjective, but ultimately they should be able to tell you whether or not the project is worth pursuing further. Metrics could include:

1. The number of individuals who indicate that they would pay for or use your product.
2. The number of individuals who state how much they would pay for your product under the pricing model you've indicated.

Priority Access

One way to gain access to users to collect their feedback is to offer priority access to those who sign up for your MVP. Priority access gives certain users a chance to use the service before everyone else. When an individual signs up, he should receive e-mail confirmation that includes a semipersonal message that says something along the lines of:

"If you want to learn more and gain priority access, please respond to this e-mail. The founders of the company will get the response. We promise it's not a black hole and we will get back to you."

By doing this you get to home in on users who clearly want your product and want it now. Many people will sign up, but by opening yourself up to potential conversations with those who request priority access you can get the feedback you need.

The Success and Failure Scenarios

Every MVP has three possible outcomes: success, partial success, and failure. Of course, every entrepreneur want his MVP to be a success, but the truth is that a good number of MVPs result in failure. Here's how to judge which category your MVP falls into.

SUCCESS

The way to determine whether an MVP is successful is fairly straightforward. If you are overwhelmed with demand for your product and people want it yesterday, then you should obviously proceed with your idea and turn it into a legitimate product. If your pricing and business model metrics start to become apparent through feedback, then you are also ahead. A potential customer who says she wants the product is one thing. A potential customer who is willing to sign a letter of intent that outlines the terms of usage puts the potential customer on a completely different level.

PARTIAL SUCCESS

This is the most likely scenario for your MVP. Partial success is defined as finding out that your product is going after a legitimate and painful problem, but the solution the MVP proposes is not what potential customers want to use. The best option here is to dig in deeper with the customer to find out what the optimal solution is. This can be dangerous, however, if it leads you to create something you don't believe in or aren't passionate about. Even if the problem stays the same, make sure the apparent solution is something you will truly want to build into a company over the next few years.

FAILURE

This is the worst scenario, but it's better to recognize that your idea has failed sooner rather than later. Your MVP falls into the failure bucket if there is lukewarm reaction, little growth, or no direct outreach from potential customers.

Don't confuse failure with lack of hustle. Before considering the MVP a failure, make sure you have spoken with enough people. Many entrepreneurs just leave feedback to chance and assume it won't come. When it doesn't, they then assume the idea is a bad one and chalk it up to failure. But no feedback does not necessarily mean bad feedback. It may just mean you need to work on getting your MVP out there a bit more.

How Cloudomatic Did It

We came up with a fairly straightforward way to decide what we would consider a success and what would indicate failure: Either developers would be breaking down our doors to use our product or they wouldn't. Here's how we looked at the different scenarios for success and failure:

FAILURE

Of course, if no one wanted the product we would know we had failed. This seemed unlikely, however, and we determined that a better indication of failure would be if users wanted the product but weren't willing to pay for it. If they thought they could build it themselves or didn't think it would offer enough value for the price they would have to pay, we wouldn't have a viable product.

PARTIAL SUCCESS

Partial success for Cloudomatic would mean that potential customers would see the value in what we were trying to offer, but would not want the product we intended to build. One big worry we had before collecting feedback was whether potential customers would find enough flexibility in our product. If they didn't, then we would have to build a fairly complex product that would be hard to architect. Our goal was to get in contact with as many customers as possible so that we could turn partial success into full success.

SUCCESS

Success to us would mean having a ton of potential customers beating down our doors to get the product. We also defined success by how much feedback we received, because we wanted to know how the product would fit in with our potential customers' workflows. If someone was not only willing to use the product but to give us their time to make it better, then we knew we were on to something.

STEP 2: POLISH E-V-E-R-Y-T-H-I-N-G

An MVP is the first impression your product will make on the world, so you need to make sure everything is as polished and professional as possible. Just because something is being put up in a weekend does not mean it can be shoddy. Consider what follows the checklist of things you should make sure are picture perfect. Many of the items may seem obvious, but these are usually the easiest to overlook.

All Copy Has Perfect Spelling and Grammar

Whether it's from a multibillion-dollar company or a simple MVP, nothing smells of unprofessionalism like lazy language. If you write less and stay consistent in your messaging, your grammar and spelling mistakes should be cut to a minimum.

If you are working on the MVP with others, make sure that they read through the site copy.

Social Media Identities Are Set Up

Normally, social media identities on Twitter and Facebook shouldn't matter when you don't even have a finished product. Don't look at them as potential traffic drivers or promotional tools, but as ways to indicate that you are serious about your product. The average user will see your presence on these sites as an indication that you are trying to communicate seriously with the world.

All Contact Methods Work and Have a Receipt

All your e-mail addressees, contact forms, and phone numbers should be working perfectly. Many people will be skeptical about a new product at first, so you need to make sure there is some form of receipt integrated on contact. In the case of a contact form, make sure you have a response set up. In the case of a telephone number, make sure you have a voicemail system.

Screenshots Are Clear and Consistent

Your screenshots should be clear and consistent. Each screenshot should aim to tell a specific part of a story and all associated screenshots should be a part of the larger story. You should include the same icons on each screenshot and make sure features appear where and how they're supposed to. If people notice inconsistencies, they won't take the product seriously. The screenshots should also be clearly labeled and indicate what a potential user is seeing.

Every Single Page Works

Every single page should work and be complete. I know this sounds obvious, but it's easy to overlook a small section of the FAQ page or an e-mail address on the contact page. Go through every single page on your MVP's site and check every detail. You should also make sure that any external and internal links work.

How Cloudomatic Did It

We made a checklist of everything listed above and checked each page carefully to make sure everything was in order. We also sent an early version to some close friends who critiqued items that didn't read right or had inconsistencies.

STEP 3: LAUNCHING THE PRODUCT AND GETTING INITIAL BUZZ

This is the big moment for the MVP and what will ultimately decide whether you should turn it into a real startup. Here's a rough timeline to follow when looking at how to take your MVP live and get initial feedback around it. This section is only about launching an MVP; to learn more about launching a full-blown product, see Chapter Six, and the story of Onswipe's first year in the appendix.

Decide a Specific Weekday and Time to Put It Live

Having a key deadline will keep you focused on working toward that day. Most people will say, "It's ready when it's ready," but that only allows you to put things off instead of making them a priority. You should have the MVP ready in a weekend, but you do not have to put it live by Monday. You should do it within ten days and have it go live on a weekday—after you have completed the steps listed below.

Allow a Twenty-four-Hour Period to Make Sure Everything Works

You should have a twenty-four-hour waiting period before going to anyone with the MVP. Things always break, even simple Web sites with nothing but screenshots and copy. Make sure the MVP is stable before promoting it to the world. You may have double-checked everything, but waiting a day and checking one more time can only help. You can never be too careful.

Reach Out to Niche and Specific Influencers

Once the twenty-four-hour waiting period has passed, you should start to reach out to niche and specific influencers about the product. An example might be a well-known blogger or personality in the fashion space if your product is fashion related. The goal is to go for quality over quantity. Make sure to approach people who can give you a seal of approval in your target market. Influencers can also give you a ton of valuable feedback. They can include industry-specific press and bloggers, authoritative individuals, and companies that could become anchor customers.

Start Reaching Out Personally to Potential Customers

There is no way around hustle when it comes to startups. Influencers may be able to help you reach a good range of individuals, but you should have a target list of five to ten potential customers you would love to receive feedback from. Influencers are not always customers themselves, but can also be those who influence the actual customer, such as members of the trade press. The list should be diversified as well, so you get a wide range of feedback from different customer types. A good list of potential customers to reach out to include:

- Large enterprise customers
- Fast-moving and young, up-and-coming companies
- Those who might be using a competitor's product
- Tech-savvy and ahead-of-the-curve potential customers who could become great evangelists for the company
- Specific forward-thinking individuals inside a company

How Cloudomatic Did It

We spent a lot of time planning how the product would launch. Cloudomatic was already up and running, so we had a small loyal following. The Cloudomatic(flow) project was not anticipated by anyone, so we thought we could fly under the radar. Boy, were we wrong.

On the Monday after we built the MVP, we made the decision to put the product live right away, and we used that day to get things settled and clear. We set a specific launch date and time of Tuesday at 3 P.M. You want to make sure you have set a specific date and time to execute on the launch.

We thought we would have a little more than twenty-four hours to make sure the MVP was okay and could be run by some close friends for a quick second glance. The 3 P.M. deadline was fairly comfortable, but we would soon be overcome by the demands of the market.

We planned to reach out to some friends via Hacker News, a niche audience of Web developers, starting at 3 P.M. the following Thursday and had a call scheduled with a VC fund at 1 P.M. on the day of the launch. As it turned out, someone who had been following the company had discovered the product through an early leak on our Facebook page and had submitted it to Hacker News before our launch time. We were off to the races and getting a ton of feedback right away. People wanted our product so badly that they leaked it to the press out of sheer excitement and word spread quickly. This helped us feel we were moving toward a successful outcome.

Because of all the attention, we had a good list of potential customers, people who had already visited the site, to reach out to from Day One. We called the ones who had given us their contact information and were instantly getting feedback from them on the needs of the product.

STEP 4: PAID USER TESTS

Sometimes the best way to get feedback is to pay for it. Since this book is about staying ultralight, I've listed suggestions that should cost no more than two hundred dollars. If you do them right, this little bit of money can go a long way to getting feedback from real individuals.

Amazon Mechanical Turk

Amazon Mechanical Turk is a wonderful hidden gem in the startup world. It allows startups to pay individuals referred to them by the site to complete short tasks that a computer could not complete, for way under a dollar and sometimes for pennies. Tasks usually include things like identifying the objects in a picture, transcribing a visual piece of media, and other repeatable tasks. In your case, the microtask should be a small survey about your MVP. The goal is to obtain user feedback on specific areas of your product before you move ahead with the real thing.

WHY IT MATTERS

Amazon Mechanical Turk matters because you can pay a small amount of money to get direct feedback from a large group of individuals. If you tried to run a survey to a large number of people on your own, it would take a ton of time and a ton of resources. Using Amazon Mechanical Turk, you can poll one hundred people for one hundred dollars and get direct insight into how you can improve your MVP.

HOW TO GET STARTED

1. Head over to www.mturk.com/mturk/welcome and sign up for an account. If you already have an Amazon account, you can use the same login and payment information.

2. Sign up as a requester, not a worker. As a requester, you are taking on the role and responsibility of asking others—the workers—to complete tasks.

3. Create a Human Intelligence Task (HIT). If you click on the Design tab, a good group of templates will be provided to you. The best one to use in this case is the Survey template.

4. Once you select the Survey template, you will be asked to specify some properties about your HIT, such as its title and description. These are pretty straightforward, but be sure to come up with a good, accurate title and description so that workers will know what is involved. Set the time limit to under ten minutes so the task doesn't sound daunting.

5. You will also be asked to state how much you are going to pay your workers and how many workers you want to complete the task. You should pay workers under a dollar and aim to get at least one hundred workers. Naturally, the more you pay the more incentivized workers will be.

6. Now you can design and deploy your template. You'll be asked what types of responses you want to receive (e.g., yes or no, multiple choice, or free format). As your

main goal is to find out whether the people completing the survey understood and agreed with your value proposition, I recommend using multiple choice questions. Some questions, like how much they would be willing to pay for your product, should be an open response.

7. Once you've set up the survey, you need to monitor the results. You can either do this in real time as workers complete the survey or come back later to look at the results. You can accept and reject results, so you don't have to pay for poorly completed survey questions.

Consumer-based startups with mainstream appeal would benefit from a Mechanical Turk survey rather than startups for niche business uses.

Guided User Testing

Guided user testing is more advanced than Amazon Mechanical Turk in terms of how specific you can get with someone taking a survey. It still allows you to be fairly hands off, but it lets you have more granular control and deeper insight into the process of how a user interprets your MVP. There are two ways to make use of this method. The first is to use an online service called UserTesting, in which users are digitally recorded as they perform actions according to a specific list of tasks that you outlined. When the user test is complete, you get a video of the person playing around with your product.

The second option is to do in-person user testing using Craigslist or some other online posting service to advertise for participants who agree to walk through your test and discuss their reactions with you one-on-one. The expected budget for this kind of test should be anywhere from one hundred dollars to two hundred dollars. You are given a video of the user going through your MVP, along with answers to the survey questions that you provided.

Guided user testing won't generate as many individual responses as Mechanical Turk, but the responses will be deeper. In-person user testing is especially useful if you are developing a specialized product that requires a very specific audience.

WHY IT MATTERS

Guided user testing lets you understand what someone is thinking when he uses your product. Mechanical Turk shows you responses from a survey, but guided user testing allows you to monitor user behavior and actions, which will give you a more accurate idea of how people respond.

HOW TO GET STARTED WITH GUIDED USER TESTING

At present, the cost of a basic trial through UserTesting is $29 per person. So for under $100 you can get three in-depth recorded sessions. You need to provide two things:

1. **Actions for a user to take while going through your MVP.** These actions should represent the natural progression a person might follow when using your product, from the home page all the way to the sign-up page. You will then be able to monitor their usage of your Web site as if they were a normal visitor, not someone paid to take a survey.

2. **Survey questions.** These should be similar to the ones you provided on Amazon Mechanical Turk, but more focused on actual site usage instead of demand for the product and market viability. For example, you might ask something like, "What confused you the most while using the site?" or "What grabbed your attention the most?"

If you opt to do in-person user testing, you'll probably have to spend more money since you need to convince people to show up in person. Fifty dollars for one hour should do it, and, again, three such tests will give you a lot of valuable feedback. You can use the same template of actions and survey questions that you would for UserTesting. The only difference is the real-time feedback from the user. Take advantage of the fact that someone is sitting right in front of you and delve deeper into her answers if you are not satisfied with her initial response.

Google AdWords

Google AdWords is the original way to generate and measure demand for an MVP. It lets you bid for advertising against certain terms that a user will search for on Google. By hyper-targeting the terms you are advertising against, you can attract the right people to your site and then gather data on how they interact with your MVP.

WHY IT MATTERS

The best thing about Google AdWords is its ability to target an audience that has shown interest in your product since the sample ad you create is matched up with a related search term that a person has entered into Google. Google AdWords is a much more objective way of looking at whether a person has an interest in your MVP in comparison to Mechanical Turk or guided user testing since you are not guiding how the user interacts with your site. It also allows you to see whether a person signed up after clicking on your ad or learn where they got lost in the process.

HOW TO BEST USE GOOGLE ADWORDS

There are four basic steps to deploying a campaign and measuring results with Google AdWords:

1. **Deciding on the copy.** The copy of your ad should consist of two main parts: a headline and two lines of text. The headline should grab the reader and include the keyword you are targeting. The text should describe your product and encourage readers to come to your site. You have ninety-five characters total, so make them count!

2. **Figuring out keywords.** The keywords you choose to target should be very specific. Remember, you're targeting a key set of potential customers and that is more important than attracting a bunch of people to your site who aren't interested. In addition, since you're bidding against other people, if you target more generic terms you will end up competing on very high-priced keywords.

3. **Setting the budget.** The amount you spend on an Ad-Words test should be somewhere between one hundred

dollars and two hundred dollars (though it's easy to find vouchers for fifty dollars to one hundred dollars off if you look around the Internet a bit). But the amount primarily depends on how much you are willing to spend for a click on a keyword, which is often referred to as the cost per click (CPC). Luckily, when selecting your keywords and setting your budget, Google will prompt you with a suggested CPC price. The higher you set your CPC, the more frequently and prominently your ad will be shown. The best way to stretch your dollar in the case of an MVP is to get as many eyeballs as possible, so you should bid on lower-priced keywords. This process will change once you have built the full product. At that stage, you'll want to use better keywords that will attract real paying customers.

4. **Measuring data.** The best way to measure data is to implement Google Analytics into your pages. This is as simple as embedding a line of code. First be sure that the e-mail address you use for your Google Analytics account is the same as the one on your Google AdWords account. Then set up a goal and a funnel for your MVP. The goal is some form of conversion, such as whenever someone signs up with an e-mail address. The funnel is the process a person goes through in order to reach that goal. The majority of visitors will not reach the conversion goal, so the funnel provides great insight into where a user drops off in the process. Setting up a Google Analytics funnel is not an easy process, but it's well worth the effort. To learn more about it, visit www.google.com/analytics.

STEP 5: HOW TO ACT ON FEEDBACK

This is the final step of the MVP and the bridge between testing the market and turning your idea into a real startup. There are a few key things that you should do in order to properly act on feedback:

FIGURE OUT HOW TO TURN AN UNSUCCESSFUL OUTCOME INTO A SUCCESS

If the MVP is not an immediate success, it does not necessarily mean that you should abandon the product right away. Perhaps you've landed on a good problem to attack but came up with the wrong solution. If this is the case, try to figure out where things went wrong. Set up a thirty-day plan to see if you can collect enough feedback to find the right solution to the problem.

FIND KEY POTENTIAL CUSTOMERS TO TALK WITH CONSTANTLY

After the feedback people, you should have a set of five to ten potential customers who you should be in constant conversation with while building the product. They will not only give you feedback but also be your champions over time. Offer them an incentive in the form of early access to the product, free access for a long time, and/or the ability to shape the product with their feedback. This small group of potential customers should help you figure out what to charge and what metrics to use.

BUILD A ROAD MAP FOR RELEASING THE PRODUCT

By building your MVP, you have laid the groundwork for making your product a reality. Now that you've got useful feedback, go back to your MVP and figure out what you need to do in order to build the first functional version of the product, which you can charge for and get some real initial traction with.

How Cloudomatic Did It

We had a good feeling that the product would be successful and our naive determination had us planning next steps from the start. We knew we needed to be ready to go to market fast.

We thought we would end up in the middle of the road and would need to rethink how to make the product work better for our target market, but our MVP was a resounding success. Luckily, our own experiences as software developers gave us great insight into the needs of our target market, so our gut instincts turned out to be right and we were ready to move on to the next step right away.

We were on the phone with key potential customers within forty-eight hours of the announcement and were getting real feedback and valuable advice. The points of confusion we had were soon made clear and resolved as we planned a first release version of the product. We also got valuable feedback on what to charge customers and what metrics to use.

We took the spec we created for the wireframes and screenshots and immediately got to work on the product. The basic gist is this: Startups are a marathon, not a sprint. Just because your MVP is over does not mean that momentum should slow down at all. We had recruited a small group to help. (You will learn more about how to bring on great talent on the cheap in Chapter Five.)

The MVP for Cloudomatic ended up going better than we ever anticipated. Its existence was leaked out to the developer community, not for malicious reasons, but because developers wanted to see this product so badly. We built the full product, but before it was released we sold the technology aspects to a competing startup. Why? We realized it would be impossible to focus on both Cloudomatic(flow) and our new venture, On-swipe, at the same time.

SUCCESSFUL COMPANIES THAT WERE STARTED IN A WEEKEND

Despite the hundreds of Startup Weekend events and thousands of hackathons that take place across the globe—not to mention the countless individuals who launch a product for fun—most projects that are started in a weekend, sadly, don't turn into anything major. Don't be discouraged if the product you set out to build in a weekend isn't quite everything you were hoping for. The skills learned are well worth the time and energy that you put forward. To keep you motivated, here are some success stories of companies that were launched over a weekend.

GROUPME

GroupMe was started and brought to market in a weekend by Steve Martocci and Jared Hecht at the 2010 *TechCrunch* Disrupt: NY Hackathon. The product is a simple way for groups to text message together. Steve and Jared turned the weekend project into a full-time startup after seeing it take off. It now has millions of users and has raised over ten million dollars in funding.

FOODSPOTTING

Foodspotting was actually started at a Startup Weekend event. It is a simple application that allows individuals to take photos of food they love with their smartphone. The product has raised over three million dollars in venture capital in under two years and has multiple millions of users.

ZAARLY

Zaarly is a marketplace to connect local buyers and sellers of services like picking up groceries or fixing things around the house. Like Foodspotting, the idea was hatched over a weekend at a Startup Weekend event in Los Angeles. The product started to gain traction and quickly became a full-time gig for its founders. Three weeks after the event, Zaarly raised one million dollars from the founders of Groupon and from Ashton Kutcher.

The key takeaway from this chapter and from the companies above is simple: Build something you want to see in the world and build it fast. Sure, it might not be perfect at first, but that's okay. There is always a next step and your work is never done.

4

GETTING ORGANIZED

NOW THAT YOU have an idea that you want to turn into a real company, it's time to become a real company. But before you move forward, you need to get organized. When you are moving a million miles an hour, the things most often on your mind are big picture items like product, financing, and hiring, but it's the simple things, the details, that can often kill a startup.

GETTING YOUR LEGAL DOCUMENTS IN ORDER

A simple disclaimer: I am not a lawyer, nor am I in any position to give legal advice. The things outlined below are important from my perspective as a founder who knows that having clean legal documentation is essential for growing a company. It makes things like raising money happen faster. Getting your legal documents in order might seem like a simple task that can be done on a whim or "when things start going well," but doing it now will make it easier to do three key things down the line:

1. **Secure venture financing.** As you will find out in Chapter Ten, raising money is a long and arduous process, during which venture capital firms will want to do due diligence on you to make sure they're making a good investment. By having your legal documents in perfect order, you make it easier for your VC's legal counsel to verify that your company is in good legal standing. If your documents are not in order when you go for venture financing the entire process may take two to three times as long.

2. **Scaling the business.** As your company grows, you'll often need legal documentation before you can hire new employees or even do something as simple as open a bank account. Make sure you have your legal documents in order so that these mundane tasks don't become complicated.

3. **Staying clean for potential acquirers.** If you are ever in a position to sell your company, you will need to have every single legal document in order before a potential acquirer will make an offer. You won't be ready to sell for a while and the acquisition process will involve many complex documents not mentioned in this book. But during the due diligence process, a potential buyer's lawyers will look through many of the documents that are created in the early days of the company, so it makes sense to get these right from the start. If you do not do this,

they will be harder to get right further down the road.

The basic legal documents include but are not limited to things such as incorporation, founders agreements, and intellectual property ownership agreements. It only costs a few hundred dollars online to incorporate your company, but this is not an area you want to be cheap on. On the other hand, you probably don't have five thousand dollars to spend on legal fees, so how does a scrappy entrepreneur go about incorporation properly without getting in a hole?

The thing to do is to find a law firm that specializes in technology and high-growth startups. If you work with a law firm from the start, you might be able to defer the basic legal fees until after you raise your first bit of capital. Many firms are willing to defer fees for things like incorporation because they assume that when you do raise money you will use them for legal services. Many of them will agree to do this because it does not take them a ton of time to execute this work. In addition, the cost of incorporation is a drop in the bucket compared to the commissions they'll earn from helping you come up with partner agreements and venture financing.

The best way to have a firm agree to defer fees is to get a reference from a current client of theirs. For Onswipe, we used Gunderson Dettmer, which has offices in Silicon Valley and New York. We chose them not only because they had completed more venture financings in the past year than anyone else, but because they were down to earth, unlike most lawyers. They were the types of lawyers you would grab a beer with.

HOW TO INCORPORATE YOUR COMPANY

Incorporation is the process of making your company a legal entity. Incorporation can come in various flavors, but the three most popular among startups are:

C Corporation. A C Corporation is the most basic form of corporation and is the form most large entities take on. After you raise outside capital, you'll probably want to convert your incorporation status to C Corporation, but it is usually not chosen by entrepreneurs at first, as it can mean double taxation, which is not favorable to a bootstrap startup. Double taxation is something to watch out for as it means you will be taxed not only at the corporate level but also at the personal level.

S Corporation. This is the most popular corporate structure for a startup as it allows the structure of a C Corp but does not require taxation at the entity level. You should use this early on to avoid double taxation.

LLC. An LLC is the simplest entity when it comes to incorporation, but it also has the least structure. There are no tax benefits to forming an LLC over a corporation. LLCs do not have shareholders and shares of stock, just members and units. Though LLCs are simpler at first, they may not allow for the flexibility you will need going forward with a startup.

Founder-Related Documents

Founder-related documents lay out the relationship that both you and your cofounder(s) have with your company. These documents should cover things like termination rights, vesting, equity splits, who sits on the board, and other things. The first thing to do before proceeding with any actual legal work is to make sure you are on the same page with your cofounder(s). Have a discussion about what you think is fair and then put it in writing.

Equity Division

The most important conversation to have with your cofounder(s) involves how equity will be distributed among all of you. Equity is the amount of ownership you have in a company. It can be measured in the amount of shares you own, which for simplicity's sake is usually thought of in percentages in the early days of the company. For example, when referring to their equity many founders will say, "I own 30 percent of the company." It's easy to put this discussion off until later or until the business finally takes off, but doing so misaligns expectations and often leads to ugly fights down the line that can not only ruin relationships but potentially threaten future venture financings because of the unstable nature of the company. There is no right way to divide up equity. Some cofounders go with a 50/50 split, while others go with 75/25, or 40/40/20 if there is a third cofounder. There is no set formula for determining what the equity split should be, but some factors to take into account are:

- Did one founder join earlier than another?
- Who has contributed the most to the product?
- Is anyone taking a larger risk than anyone else?
- Who came up with the idea?
- Has anyone left his job to join the startup?

Vesting

The vesting period also gives the cofounders a stake in the company by ensuring that they are compensated for work they have already completed as well as for work they will complete in the future. This is the simplest way to protect the company in case a cofounder or employee leaves. The most typical vesting schedule provides for a one-year "cliff" followed by three years of monthly vesting. A cliff is the period during which an employee must stay with the company in order to get any equity at all. If a cofounder leaves before the cliff period ends they do not receive any compensation. After the cliff period ends they start earning equity on a monthly basis for the next three years. After the full four-year vesting period, all the stock belongs to the founder.

For example, let's say you're offering your cofounder 40,000 shares in the company with a one-year cliff for 25 percent followed by three years monthly for the remaining 75 percent. This means that after one year he would own 10,000 shares, but if he left after nine months to pursue another venture he would own nothing. After one year he would start earning 833.33 shares per month for the next three years (30,000 shares divided by 36 months).

Though you don't have to figure this out the second you decide to partner with someone, you should set the groundwork for vesting before you start raising capital from serious outside investors, so when the money starts coming in you'll know how it is to be allocated. In order to complete the financing, investors will most likely ask that you modify your vesting schedule or add a brand new one to protect the company. No matter what you do, each cofounder should be on the same vesting schedule in order to keep things equal. Having a different vesting schedule for different cofounders sets a bad precedent for employees in the future. It also gives one cofounder the ability to leave earlier than another while still getting ownership in the company.

83(b) Election

Making an 83(b) election is by far the most commonly overlooked—and potentially financially disastrous—decision a founder can make. So pay attention! 83(b) elections ensure that you are not paying a large sum of money on taxes on the difference between the value of the stock when you first start the company and the value when it vests.

As a founder, the par value (or face value) of your stock is probably a fraction of a penny—let's say 1¢. At the end of your one-year cliff you will purchase stock at this value, not at it's current value, which let's say is now $1. If you do not make an 83(b) election, you will pay the taxes on the difference between the two values, which in this case is 99¢. Stock prices for founders are kept very low as the shares should cost almost nothing for a founder to buy once they are vested. By filing an 83(b) election, you will not be taxed on the increase in price. In short, do you want to be paying taxes on a penny or on a dollar?

Intellectual Rights Agreements for Employees and Contractors

You may assume that if you pay someone for completing a job related to your company, you own all the work they produce in the process. That is not true. Fortunately, there are simple steps you can take to make sure you own the intellectual property rights to what your employees and contractors deliver to you.

The first documents to get in order are those that outline the rights the company owns for any work produced by you or your cofounders. These ensure that if any disagreements come about that cause a cofounder to leave the company, everything he or she has built still belongs to the company. This is especially important when it comes to your tech cofounder, though the rights should be the same for all cofounders.

After you've outlined the intellectual property terms among the cofounders, you should do the same for all your other employees and contractors. Standard terms often include making sure that any work done and its derivatives are the property of the company. Your goal here is not to own a coworker's soul but to make sure that work they do for you and your company belongs solely to you and cannot be reused. Before any real work is done, make sure they have looked at and signed a Proprietary Information and Inventions Agreement (PIIA). This document outlines your rights as a startup to the work that anyone else may do for you.

Another point of contention in the technology industry is the use of noncompete clauses. Noncompetes are unenforceable in California, which is where many startups are situated.

But in some states, such as Massachusetts, noncompetes can be enforced by startups. As a founder you should look into noncompetes not only relative to your startup, but also to make sure you are not breaching a previous noncompete that you may have signed with a current or previous employer.

STAYING ORGANIZED WITH THE FIVE DIVISIONS RULE

When you're first starting out as an entrepreneur, it's easy to get excited and begin working on many different things at one time with no clear answer as to how any of them fit into the business. When things start moving fast, you will not be able to go full throttle on everything at once; you will have to pick and choose what to focus on in order to reach your current goal. The easiest way to do this is by using the Five Divisions Rule.

I developed the Five Divisions Rule while at Onswipe. Basically, it forces you to look at your business in terms of five distinct categories: product, business development and sales, public relations and marketing, finance and funding, and hiring and HR. The optimal number of divisions to go full throttle on is two, though three can work well. By looking at the business through the lens of these five divisions, you'll not only be able to stay more focused, you'll also be able to communicate more effectively with those to whom you report (investors) and those who report to you (employees).

Product

The product division of your company involves both your big picture strategy for building your product as well as what you need to do on a day-to-day basis in order to reach your goal. Since your product is the core of your business, it's extremely important from the beginning to outline the process for developing it and set deadlines that will help you achieve various goals. Consider this division the equivalent of project management, but at a very high level. Here are the three things you should always have organized:

1. **Quarterly road map.** Every three months you should draw up a road map to outline your goals for the upcoming quarter. It should be very in-depth and have hard dates associated with building out the product. At this point you are probably building the first version of your product from the MVP, so it's key to set deadlines for a first version for internal review, aka beta version, a private launch, and a public launch.

2. **Rest of the year road map.** Although it's important to have specific goals outlined for the quarter, you should also figure out what you want to build for the rest of the year. These are the big picture ideas that you want to execute in the future but do not have the resources or mindshare to start thinking about right now. For this plan, it's more important to focus on the what, not the when.

3. **Future brainstorm.** Along the way, you will have a ton of ideas about products you want to build far out

into the future. Instead of acting on the ideas too early and becoming unfocused or disregarding the ideas entirely, set them aside in a future product brainstorm list.

Business Development and Sales

I'll talk at length about the business development process in several later chapters, but right now it's important to figure out how to keep your business development funnel organized so you can keep track of potential leads and of where you are in the business cycle. The best way to do this is to:

Set the funnel. The funnel is the list of potential customers you are going after. The top of the funnel, which is wide, encompasses those customers you have just started to talk to. The middle of the funnel, which is narrower, encompasses those customers you are in negotiations with but may or may not close with. At the bottom of the funnel are customers you have almost closed with and who require the most intense focus. Set the funnel early on so your operations are clearly organized, and so you know how to organize the conversations that you are having with potential customers. This should always be the first step to an organized business development process.

Prioritize inbound leads. If you execute your MVP well enough, you will start to receive a number of inbound leads. You don't have to respond immediately, but prioritize the ones you feel are most important and put the rest aside to be contacted at a later date.

Organize outbound leads. From the time you start building your product you should have a wish list of potential customers and partners you want to reach out to. It will take months and possibly even a year to reach all of them, but keep a detailed, organized list of dream customers and work your way through them as you can.

Organize ongoing conversations. Although it's important to stay in touch with leads, it's easy to lose track of where you are in the conversation and when to follow up. Figure out a system for appropriately timing conversations and don't forget to update your funnel to reflect your progress.

PR and Marketing

Good PR requires planning and a great amount of coordination with the way you plan to release your product to the public. The PR schedule should be dependent upon your product schedule, and the two will work in sync very heavily .

You should have a monthly or bimonthly PR milestone to work toward and you need to make sure that it is planned in advance. The milestone might be a new product release or it might be a full-blown press event. You should also keep a running list of press mentions, which will help your progress over time. You can also share this list with new hires as a way to get them excited about the progress of the company and to get their perspective of the company's growth.

You should also have a marketing plan that includes strategies such as content marketing, conference talks, and other general ways to create buzz. Here are a few initiatives that we have started at Onswipe to make sure buzz is constantly going:

- **Highlighting customers.** Every week we highlight customers who have come onto the platform and show them off on our blog.
- **Monthly infographics.** We send out monthly infographics to our e-mail list to keep the market updated as to what is happening with our product.
- **Speaking gigs.** I try to speak at a conference at least once a month in order to educate and meet new people.

A key practice that many startups fail to do is organizing their messaging to the public. Every startup should always have the following things in their arsenal:

- **A one-liner.** You need to be able to describe what your product does in one line or less. It should be a simple way for people to get what you do. At Onswipe, our tagline is "Insanely Easy Tablet Publishing."
- **Three-sentence additional pitch.** This should expand on the one-liner and convey an operational sense of what you do.
- **Current product push overview.** At any given time you should be pushing a specific feature-set of your product. As you release new features, you should have the value propositions associated with those features down pat. At Onswipe, we added advertising early on since the value to the publisher meant increased revenue.

Finance and Funding

This division can be broken down into two areas: the way you spend money and the way you raise money from outside investors. Since you probably won't have a lot of capital to spend when you're first starting out, you'll need to focus on the funding side of things for a while.

When it comes to funding, plan and organize your conversations with current investors as well as potential ones. As a general rule, you should start raising money six months before cash runs out since it may take a while to raise what you need. This may vary significantly depending on the funding market. In a bullish market you may be able to raise funding in a matter of weeks, whereas in a bear market it can take months.

Once you have earned money, you need to plan how to spend it. Accounting is difficult to deal with and as a founder you don't want to add any other stress to your plate that will take your focus away from the product. So take some time to set up a simple accounting system like QuickBooks to keep track of your startup's financial health. As you start spending money, ask yourself these two questions on a biweekly basis: What is currently your biggest cost? How are you spending money? You should always be on the lookout for ways you can cut costs.

Hiring and HR

There are two sides to the hiring coin: taking on new employees and retaining current ones. At first it will likely be yourself, a cofounder, and maybe some freelancers, but as the company starts to grow so will your staff—and it will happen fast. At Onswipe we went from two people to twenty within our first year. Twenty people may still not seem like a lot, but when you're growing at a rate of ten times a year, it can be a lot to handle.

If you do not have any capital raised yet, you will have to offer early employees significant equity stakes. The less capital you havé to give in the early days, the more equity you will have. Giving away equity with very little cash is a lot more work. Even though you may see the value in equity, the people you are trying to hire may not see the same value in it. If you have raised capital you may have money, but you still have to be selective with your choices. You should start planning out who you want to hire three, six, and twelve months in the future and what it will require on two spectrums: equity and salary. A few rules about how to stay organized and when to hire:

- **Hire according to the road map.** Don't just hire at random and then place people somewhere with not much to do.
- **Set aside an equity pool.** This is usually 10 percent to 15 percent of your equity that you set aside for new employees. When you receive venture financing, it is often mandatory.
- **Never more than double your number of employees every six months.** This rule will help you grow your company in proportion to its current size. At a certain point there are diminishing returns to hiring more people, and it also takes a lot of work for a founder and executive to grow a team that fast.

■ **You should now have your documents in order for yourself, your cofounders, and the company.** This is a boring and tedious process but it is useful as it has set you up for when you hire new employees.

Of course, before you start negotiating with new employees, you need to figure out how, when, and who to hire, which is what we'll discuss in the following chapter.

5

YOU CAN'T GO IT ALONE

NO ONE CAN grow a startup entirely on his own and at some point you will have to start bringing people into your team and working with outside parties. You should do this as soon as you begin to feel overwhelmed and need to delegate tasks to others.

Investors will look at three key factors when considering a startup for potential investment: people, product, and market. When I first started courting investors, I assumed a large market was the most important factor and that the other two were secondary. But I was wrong . . . very wrong. People are the most important asset of a startup. They breed perseverance, come up with great ideas, and let you build for the long haul and ultimately succeed. Once you have great people on board with what you're doing, everything else will fall into place over time.

This chapter focuses on how to bring great people into your startup effectively. The most important person is your cofounder, because whoever you choose will be your other half over the next few years. There are two types of cofounders. One is focused on the technology and the other is focused on the business. That is, one builds the product while the other sells the product. Below you will find great traits for both types of cofounders. Don't skip over the section that describes you, as it will give you good insight into how to be better at whatever role you're in. After you find a great cofounder you can focus on hiring your first employees and using freelancers to get things done fast with little capital.

THE TECHNICAL COFOUNDER

If you come from a business background, you'll need to find someone with solid technical knowledge to be your cofounder.

Technical cofounders are the unicorns of the startup world. They're hard to find and even harder to keep. Pretty much everyone from a business background who is looking to start a tech startup struggles to find a technical cofounder. That's because most business founders don't know what to look for. Below is a list of what's important in a technical cofounder, along with suggestions for where to look and questions to ask your potential cofounder.

A Pure Love for Building Products

A great technical cofounder will love building products just like Michael Jordan loved playing basketball. The best technical cofounders want to solve challenging problems and build things not because they have to but because they want to. When considering someone to be your tech cofounder, look at what he has built in his spare time, not just what he has built for previous employers. In a startup you are creating something that is born from your own vision. The easiest way to understand how a potential technical cofounder may operate under those conditions is by looking at what they have designed on their own. Her work for someone else does not illustrate her vision, even if she did a great job or went above and beyond.

Key Question to Ask

"What products have you built in the past two years in your spare time?"

Key Traits to Look For

- Has built many projects in the past for fun and is not afraid to show them off.
- Works to improve an idea and add a unique edge by adding or removing features.
- Has a repository on sites such as GitHub, which lets programmers show off what they have built.
- Attends hackathons or events where people gather to build things instead of just talking about building them.

An Understanding of Where Business and Technology Meet

A great technical cofounder will have a strong understanding of where well-built technology intersects with the actual business of the company. Even talented cofounders with a passion for building things will often lose sight of the overall mission of the company. If a technical cofounder starts ignoring the overall business, the greatest technological solutions will not matter. Make sure your technical cofounder realizes you are building a company, not a side project.

Key Question to Ask

"What cool feature or technology have you built that also made a big impact on the overall business?"

Key Traits to Look For

- Considers the impact a feature may have on the business as a whole instead of just adding something to add something.
- Takes pride in developing products that make money, not just those that are fun to make.
- Prioritizes features that will support paying customers.

The Ability to Attract Great Technical Talent

Your technical cofounder will be responsible for bringing in more technical talent as your revenues grow and your company raises more money over time. When looking at a potential technical cofounder, you need to consider if he will be able to attract others who are just as good, if not better.

Key Question to Ask

"Can you name two people who are as smart as you who you would want to come work for you?"

Key Traits to Look For

- Has an online following via their blog or Twitter account that includes people who might want to work for your startup.

- Knows which companies he would recruit from and why.
- Has worked at a company he can pull talent from.

Domain Expertise

I have said it before and I will say it again: Startups win on speed. By having domain expertise in the problem you are trying to solve, a startup can move way faster. Without that expertise, a technical cofounder would have to acquire knowledge on the job that a better candidate may already have through years of learning. Leveraging domain expertise and past experiences is like having your technical cofounder's past employer pay for your success.

Key Question to Ask

"What makes you better suited than anyone else to solve this specific problem?"

Key Traits to Look For

- Has worked on similar problems in the past or in a related field that would give her domain expertise.
- Is a respected source of information on solving the problem at hand.

Knows How to Say No

A good technical cofounder knows how to stay focused on the problem rather than simply trying to do whatever he knows how to do. When you are a "maker," you have a natural inclination to add just one more thing. But that one additional thing often turns into five more things that delay the entire product. By knowing how to say no, a technical cofounder makes sure that a product ships with only the necessary features.

Key Question to Ask

"What was the hardest feature to cut in a product you built and why did you decide to do it?"

Key Traits to Look For

- Questions the need for features on the product you want to build.
- Homes in on one area of what you are building.
- Starts to talk about a road map and launch strategy that focuses on a core part of what you are building.

Where to Find a Technical Cofounder

1. **Hacker News.** This is a site where entrepreneurs and programmers contribute great links on a daily basis about technology-focused entrepreneurship. You can find it at news.ycombinator.com.

2. **Local tech meetups.** Those who attend meetups have a true interest in learning. In addition, live events allow you to meet someone face-to-face before you decide if she would be a good candidate. Check out www.meetup .com for events in your area.

3. **Past or current coworkers.** If you have worked with someone before and know they have what it takes, you'll save yourself the stress of taking on a stranger.

4. **Hackathons.** Companies will often hold daylong events to build onto their existing products. These events attract great technical talent with a passion for building things. You can find them by subscribing to www.Startup Digest.com.

5. **Startup Weekends.** These are weekend-long sprints that pair strangers to crank out a prototype of a product. You can find them at startupweekend.org.

THE BUSINESS COFOUNDER

Many tech cofounders think they don't need a business cofounder, which is far from the truth. Every startup needs someone who is capable of selling the product and positioning its strategy to the outside world. Even though it's extremely difficult to find a good business cofounder, it seems as though there's a surplus of people with business backgrounds trying to enter the startup world. I think this is because it's easy to fake being a good business cofounder, but it's hard to fake being a good technical cofounder. Either you code or you don't. Nonetheless, there are certain things you should look for if you need a business cofounder.

A Knack for Hiring Great Talent

Startups depend on their people, and your business cofounder needs to know how to curate potential talent. They need to be able to find the best talent possible and get them on board with the big vision of the company.

Key Question to Ask

"What would be your process not only for finding great talent but also for qualifying them?"

Key Trait to Look For

- Has a specific process for hiring people. He shouldn't be scouring job boards but finding unique ways to hire people. At Onswipe I will often search design communities and blogs when looking for people to hire.

A Deep Knowledge of Customer Acquisition Techniques

Your startup cannot last unless people are willing to use—and, more importantly, pay for—your product. Knowing how to attract customers and scale these acquisition tactics is the key attribute of a business cofounder.

Key Question to Ask

"What are the two primary outlets you would use for acquiring customers within the first six months of the company's existence?"

Key Traits to Look For

- Knows where to look for a potential customer base.
- Is familiar with partners with whom you could cut business development deals.
- Knows how to calculate whether a customer acquisition technique can be profitable.

Can Craft a Clear and Concise Message

You may think it's easy to explain what you do to the rest of the world. But the reality is that most people won't understand it right away. One reason why this is is that people have a short attention span, but another reason is that most startups fail to communicate their message effectively. A great business co-founder will be able to translate the practical function of the startup into easily digestible sound bites people can understand.

Take a look at Twitter, a startup that many didn't understand for a while. With this confusion in the marketplace, then CEO Evan Williams took the time to turn the confusion around by clearly explaining what Twitter was: a new form of communication. Many saw Twitter as pointless, but because of Ev's direction Twitter is now seen as a communication platform for short-form bites of real-time information.

Key Question to Ask
"How would you describe the company in two sentences?"

Key Traits to Look For
- Can summarize the complex inner workings and technology of the startup using clear language that anyone can understand.
- Puts together great presentations for speaking gigs and public events.
- Can speak to the press.

Understands Your Potential Customer Base and Your Value Proposition

A great business cofounder will understand your potential customer base's needs and pain points. Odds are your cofounder saw the pain point firsthand and used to or even still does walk in the shoes of your potential users.

One way to determine if she understands your value proposition is if she dogfoods your product. "Dogfooding" is a term used in Silicon Valley to describe the act of building a product that you will use yourself, not just push on others. In other words, you will eat your own dog food. The best business cofounders will work toward building a product that they will dogfood.

Key Question to Ask

"Why do you want to use the product we want to build?"

Key Traits to Look For

- Is passionate about seeing the product brought into the world and would be one of the first users.
- Has a product background and some base technology knowledge so she can deliver value to the user.

Past Experience Pitching Investors

A great business cofounder will know how to pitch investors on the company's big vision. In fact, the best way to weed out potential business cofounders is to have them create a simple investor deck of their vision for the company after you have an initial conversation with them. This lets you see how well they can pitch and also how they interpret the vision of the company.

Another test would be to ask them to identify critical issues in the business that they think investors will look at and then ask them to come up with solutions.

Your business cofounder should also understand when it's appropriate to raise money and when it's not. Raising money too early can cause a company to accelerate too fast and raising money too late can cause a company to die.

Key Question to Ask

"How much would you raise, when would you raise it, and from whom?"

Key Traits to Look For

- Understands the basics of venture finance, including term sheets, premoney valuations, and general legal jargon.
- Understands how much your business really needs to raise and which funds would be allies for you.
- Has experience raising money in the past. This is a huge plus, but not required.

Knows How to Develop the Business

Ask a potential business cofounder the three dream deals he would cut to get your product the widest distribution possible. You should also ask what other strategic deals he has cut in the past and whether they were at a startup or a very large company.

You should also ask him about any deals he's had fall apart or not go the way he expected. By finding out where and how your potential business cofounder has failed, you are able to see how well he follows through. Anyone can start a business development deal, but getting it to go live is a whole other thing. It's the equivalent of a technical cofounder building a product but never shipping it. Real deals go live.

Key Question to Ask

"What is the most ambitious deal you would go after and why?"

Key Traits to Look For

- Prioritizes which deals to go after.
- Identifies deals that can get done fast.

Strong Product Knowledge

Your business cofounder should be a product guy. Odds are she will carry the CEO title, and the best CEOs have always been focused on building a great product.

The business cofounder should also have some level of technical understanding. That doesn't mean she should be coding all the time, but she shouldn't be afraid to get her hands dirty if she needs to. Most important, basic technical knowledge will allow her to understand how business decisions are affected by technical decisions and vice versa. Bad business cofounders will often make promises that can't be delivered on the technical side.

Key Question to Ask

"Have you ever been in a hands-on product management or software development role?"

Key Traits to Look For

- Has written specifications for a product in the past and can clearly organize a vision for what is being created.
- Has prior experience in software development, even if it's rudimentary.

Where and How to Find a Business Cofounder

The best way to find a business cofounder is to look at the business development offices at companies in your area of expertise. As an exercise, list all the companies that would be either large customers or potential acquirers of your company. From there, you can find a group of potential business cofounders.

FINDING FREELANCERS
WHO DON'T SUCK

No matter how fantastic your cofounders are, you still won't be able to grow your business without some extra help. Freelancers provide the labor capabilities of a company ten times your size without the overhead. At Onswipe we use contractors and freelancers extensively in order to turn up the speed at which a product can be shipped. With freelancers we can double our staff size for two months in order to complete a project or meet a deadline without having to worry about high HR costs or long-term commitments. The key is making sure the freelancers you find don't suck.

When to Use Freelancers

Freelancers should be used when you need a short engagement taken care of or when you need to meet a critical deadline on time or even faster. Basically, you should use them whenever you need a little extra temporary help.

Referrals Are King

The problem with freelancers is that it's difficult to know if they're reliable before you actually work with them. As you work with more and more people you'll probably develop a list of go-to freelancers you love, but until that point you should rely on fellow entrepreneurs for referrals.

To start, identify quality work at another company (preferably one where you know people) and ask if it was done by a freelancer. If so, ask the person who hired him whether he was easy to work with and how much he charged. If it seems like he might be a good match, ask to be introduced.

This process will also improve the chances that a great freelancer will work for you instead of for other companies. A lot of companies fail to pay freelancers on time or even pay them at all. If a freelancer is referred to another company by a client that has treated them well, they are much more likely to take the gig.

Cheaper Is Almost Never Better

At first you won't have a ton of cash to pay freelancers, but do not get into the trap of hiring the freelancer who costs the least. Repeat after me: *Do not get into the trap of hiring the free-*

lancer who costs the least. Great freelancers will often charge a rate higher than you expected, but it will be worth the extra expense in the long run.

Here's how a nightmare freelancer scenario might play out when you try to find the cheapest possible option:

1. Ten dollars an hour sounds absolutely awesome and the freelancer swears she can do everything for you.

2. You hire her and she gets started. She misses her first deadline by five days, but you let it slide because she's cheaper.

3. She finally provides the first deliverable, but it's not what you expected and the code to go with it is absolute junk.

4. You're frustrated, you don't hear from her for days, and the project is now thirty days past due with nothing good to show for it.

5. You eventually end up having to fire the freelancer and start from scratch . You paid her for one hundred hours of work at ten dollars an hour, which is a thousand dollar loss along with an even bigger loss in time. We brought in a freelancer at Onswipe for a quick job, but because he did not complete the task well, we had to do it all over again. We lost time and money.

More expensive freelancers can charge higher rates because they have earned respect and know people will pay for that. There is no set guideline for pricing freelancers; it depends on the task, the programming language, their location, and the overall amount of work you give them.

Push Back Is Good

You do not want to hire a yes-man or yes-woman. Although they are not full-time employees, freelancers should still have a sense of creativity and control. The best freelancers take pride in and ownership of their work, which means they might not go about things exactly the way you tell them to. Of course, a good freelancer will confer with you about any changes she wants to make, but push back should be seen as a sign that she cares, not that she's trying to be difficult. When hiring a freelancer, some questions to ask include:

1. What two things would you change about the product we have asked you to execute?

2. What does our competitor do that you think we should do?

3. Would you have your family and friends use this product?

If you can find good freelancers who go above and beyond, you will not only get your money's worth, you might even improve your product.

Freelancer Hack: Building a Workforce of One Hundred Without the Overhead

One of the biggest advantages we have at Onswipe is an extensive network of freelancers that we can call on when we need something done fast. This allows us to double our work capacity and team overnight whenever we need to. It's also a way to keep things lean since we don't have to worry about large expenses like tax withholding, health insurance, stock compensation, and moving expenses. It might take you awhile to find freelancers you trust, but it is definitely something to work toward.

Once you do build up your list, here's how to keep things organized:

1. Divide labor into different divisions.
   a. Design: The actual user interface.
   b. Front-end development: Turns the design from a Photoshop or static jpeg file to working code.
   c. Back-end development: Writes the logic that processes information. This is the work you never see.
2. Make sure all tasks are split up into clearly defined chunks that can be completed within a thirty-day period.
3. Establish a preset group of rates for each freelancer and make sure they all get paid on time. Don't set project rates. If you keep things at a per hour rate, freelancers will get things done faster. They understand that if they work faster they see the money faster.
4. Send out monthly newsletters to keep your freelancers in the loop. Let them know of upcoming projects you might need them for or just update them on the overall happenings with the product. By keeping freelancers in the loop, they will be able to dive back into your product without feeling lost

when it comes to the overall vision—even if it's been a while since they've worked with your product directly.

WHEN TO HIRE FULL-TIME EMPLOYEES

If you find you are relying on freelancers a lot, it may make sense for you to bring on full-time employees. The best way to find new employees is to draw from freelancers you love working with. At Onswipe, our lead designer started out as a freelancer, but we quickly brought him on full time.

Which Freelancers Should You Hire?

You'll work with a lot of great freelancers, but when deciding which ones to hire you should consider certain things:

HAVE THEY DEVELOPED A UNIQUE STYLE FOR YOUR PRODUCT?

Great designers and developers often have a unique style all their own that can give your product a special edge. The problem comes when the freelancer stops working for you. Sure, you can try to find a designer who will imitate that style, but it will never be as good. If a freelancer has brought a unique flavor to your startup that you want to continue using for the long term, try to bring them on permanently.

DO YOU PERSONALLY ENJOY WORKING WITH THEM?

Working with people is about relationships, and even though it's relatively easy to find someone who can work quickly and produce what you ask for, it's hard to find people you actually like to work with. If you develop a great working relationship with a freelancer, that is a good sign that they'd make a great addition to your team. It's difficult to mix business and friendship, but this is about something different. It's about having a smooth working relationship and a culture fit within the company, which is often hard to find.

WOULD YOU BE AFRAID OF THEIR WORKING FOR A COMPETITOR?

This should not be the sole reason or even a main reason to hire a freelancer, but it is a good question to ask. If you worry that a competitor could gain an edge by hiring one of your freelancers, consider whether it might be worth it to snatch her up first.

What if I Don't Have the Funds?

Hiring people is expensive and you may not have the funds at first to bring on people full time. If you know someone you would like to hire full time but can't make them the offer right away, the best thing to do is to let them know your intentions. If a freelancer knows he might get a full-time gig, he may be willing to spend more time with you on a particular project rather than seek out projects from other companies in order to stay afloat. Giving them a heads-up is also courteous because it lets them inform existing clients that they might need to hire someone else.

FINDING ADVISERS WITHOUT AN AGENDA

Advisers are an essential part of running lean as a startup because they allow you to borrow experience and get access to places that you may not be able to get to otherwise. Good advisers have years of experience and can help you avoid mistakes. Basically, they are the living, breathing, and interactive version of this book, and they can make your life way easier. Below are some tips for finding valuable advisers.

Start with Your Network

Sometimes a great adviser might be a connection away; in some cases he might be many connections away. You may need to network through multiple people to get to a potential adviser.

Fall in Love with Each Other

If someone is going to advise you on how to run your business, you have to fall in love with them—and they have to fall in love with you. They have to believe in the business and, more important, in you as its founder. They need to think the way you do and see a little bit of themselves in you. Give off the energy and emotion that will make them addicted to your personality. Be polite and kind, but also be confident.

Look for Those in Your Field

It's better to have an adviser who is an expert, not a celebrity. Stick with advisers who know your domain and are able to advise you on strategy. Advisers are oracles who can see into the future because they have been through earlier versions of the problems you have faced. Ask yourself, "What problems specific to our idea will we encounter over the next three years?" From there you should be able to identify companies that went through similar problems. Find early employees or founders of those companies to advise you. We added the former CEO of DoubleClick as an adviser since there are a lot of similarities between what we are doing with advertising in the touch space and what he built in the point-and-click world.

Take Advice from Other Entrepreneurs

You want to make sure your advisers have been in your shoes before and know the pain that comes with starting a company. Advisers that don't have entrepreneurial experience are probably not the best people to get involved with your company. You want someone who has seen all the despair you have seen and can help you cope with it.

Their Experience Can Scale as You Grow

If things really take off, your advisers should be able to grow with the company over time. At a certain point, though, they may no longer be of as much use to you as they were in the beginning. That's okay and a good problem to have. Make sure that your adviser can help you deal with initial problems like raising capital, business model development, hiring, product strategy, and dealing with incoming business development inquiries.

First Comes Love, Then Compensation

An adviser should fall in love with you and the company before figuring out what the compensation will be in terms of equity. It should never be cash. Depending upon the stage your business is in, it is reasonable to give an adviser .1 percent to .2 percent equity. Compensation discussions should happen early, but they should be mostly a formality. Compensation should not make or break whom you choose as an adviser.

Apply to TechStars

Andres and I joined the TechStars program in 2011 as part of the inaugural class in New York City. If you're willing to live in New York, this is a great program for young companies. We were a part of the New York City program, but there are also great programs in Boulder, Boston, and Seattle. With over ninety mentors from the technology sector, teams have access to advice on any specific skill set that they need, whether it's business development, technology, or public relations. It's not an easy program to get into, but it's certainly worth applying.

6

ATTRACTING
CUSTOMERS

IF YOU BUILD a product and no one uses it, does it really exist? The answer is no. Many entrepreneurs build a product assuming that users and customers will naturally materialize, but the truth is, even the best products can't attract customers without a lot of help from their founders. It's up to you to figure out the best way to bring customers in the door immediately.

There are several effective ways to acquire customers, and although all of them may not work for you, you should consider using more than one method to achieve the maximum results.

BLOGGING

Not only does blogging give you a way to keep readers abreast of updates and happenings inside the company, it also allows you to establish yourself as a thought leader and an expert in your field. The topics you cover should be ones that educate, inform, and help readers. By doing this you become a go-to adviser and your fans will often become customers. By creating interesting content you also increase the likelihood that readers will pass it on to other readers and potential customers. Consider adding videos or other visual elements like infographics that will encourage readers to pass along your content.

Example: Mint

Mint is a service that allows individuals to track and budget their personal finances better. After only three years, it was sold to Intuit for $170 million. Mint's success can be attributed not only to its amazing technology but also to its blog, which allowed the site to gain traction among users even before it launched. Mint gained this traction by employing the art of search engine optimization (more on this later) and using specific keywords and phrases that allowed them to rank high in searches for popular terms like "personal finance" without paying a ton of money for placement.

One of the smartest things the Mint blog did was to focus on a highly targeted demographic: young people. This audience has since expanded, but Mint benefited from going after the group most likely to be early adopters of new technology like theirs. Of course, older people need a product like Mint, but they are also more likely to worry about privacy and about linking their personal banking accounts to a third-party Web site. By focusing on a young crowd that could spread the word, Mint knew it could get more traction in the market.

PUBLIC RELATIONS

Public relations is the art of getting the press and journalists to write about your company. It is not only useful to know how to handle the press in good times; it is just as useful to understand how to handle the press when things go wrong.

Good PR creates favorable buzz about what your company is up to, both before and after launch. Getting good buzz requires two key things: telling a story that paints you in a good light from the start and having a great product. PR is often considered free advertising but this is far from true, as PR takes a monumental amount of effort. But if it is done right, PR can bring a large number of potential new customers in the door.

Public relations is something I spend a lot of time on and we'll explore it further later in the book.

Example: WePay

WePay is an alterative to PayPal that accepts payments online for things like rent and charity donations. Knowing it faced an entrenched competitor, WePay decided it needed to do something bold that would get massive attention from the public.

Luckily for them, PayPal is despised by most in the developer community for withholding money and freezing user accounts. Taking advantage of this pain point, WePay froze hundreds of dollars inside six hundred pounds of ice and dropped it in front of PayPal's 2010 developer conference in San Francisco. The stunt was designed to symbolize how Pay-

Pal freezes user accounts, but this was not just some random gag. WePay notified the press of what they were going to do in advance and took care to document the entire experience so they could share photos and videos later. The stunt garnered tons of national press and put WePay in the spotlight both for their ingenuity and for their product. When pulling off a PR stunt, you need to have a clear goal that you want to accomplish. Here is what we can learn from WePay's anti-PayPal stunt:

They had a goal. WePay wanted to get the attention of the thousands of developers in attendance and make them aware that a developer-friendly alternative existed.

They declared an enemy. WePay identified an enemy in the form of PayPal. Companies should only declare an enemy if their customers are truly unhappy with the competition. In WePay's case, everyone had a strong dislike for PayPal but there was no alternative to champion as a hero. They didn't engage in a smear campaign just to make themselves look good. They simply leveraged widespread unhappiness to their advantage.

They did something that got attention. Dropping six hundred pounds of ice in the middle of a developer's conference will surely get attention. Not only were people curious about what was going on, they were also curious about how the ice got there.

They documented the entire process. Everyone loves to know the story behind the story. People will want to know how the stunt was pulled off and the backstory. By documenting the entire process, you establish yourself as an authority and get more press in the process. WePay shared a ton of photos and videos from the stunt, which showed them doing everything from picking up the truck to hauling the block of ice to putting the money inside the ice to be frozen to dropping it off in front of the conference.

They notified press. WePay made sure that every press outlet knew what they were up to. They also stayed in contact to make sure the press was able to get the full story from them before, during, and after.

In the end, WePay's traffic increased considerably and they started to garner nationwide attention. How much higher did it grow? Let's take a look at the stats from a few weeks after:

- A 225 percent increase in signups
- A 300 percent increase in weekly traffic
- A threefold increase in the number of visitors to the site who converted to customers

SOCIAL SHARING

Over the past five years, Facebook and Twitter have given businesses a radical new way to gain traction. No longer do they have to rely on search engines. They can actually use other people to spread their message.

Integrating social sharing into your business encourages users to share pieces of content through their social networks.

You can achieve this by doing something as simple as including a Facebook or Twitter button on every page of your site. Below are a few ways to use social sharing effectively:

- **Have consistent placement.** Make sure that each button is clearly visible and placed in the same place on every page. If you change the placement, users will get confused and they will be less likely to use the buttons. Users may not want to use them the first time they visit, but eventually they will want to share content. By making social sharing up front, visible, and in a consistent place, users will know where to go when that time comes.

- **Make sharing part of signing up.** When users sign up for your service or subscribe to your blog, ask them if they want to share it or refer friends via social media. Make sure to sell this as a benefit to the user, not as a spammy opportunity. Sell your users on the fact that your service becomes way more useful if they get their friends involved. Don't require people to share anything, but say something like, "Spread the word! The more people who know about us, the more we can do to improve our product—and the more you get out of it! Share this link with your friends!"

- **Establish a line of trust.** Never spam a user's friends list or cross a line that violates trust. There's a fine line between integrating social sharing and abusing a user's Twitter stream or Facebook wall. Have a clear opt-in experience and make sure a user knows what they are getting into. Word spreads easily if you betray a user's trust with access to his social network.

Social sharing is pretty basic to do and will allow your startup to gain exposure as more and more users share with their friends. But to be truly effective you need to make the actions above loop in more users and become a customer acquisition machine all by itself. The goal of social sharing is to have each user bring in at least one more new user.

There is a powerful concept in social sharing known as the double viral loop, in which a user who is brought in as a consumer can also become a creator. YouTube loops in people virally through great videos that are uploaded by other users. These people came to the site because someone was kind enough to take the time to upload a video. YouTube works so well because they are able to turn a certain percentage of content consumers into content creators.

You should always be asking yourself: How can I convert those who come to my site as content consumers into content creators?

Example: Threewords.me

Threewords.me was started as a simple side project by a close friend of mine named Mark Bao. The site lets individuals post a page where friends anonymously described them in three words or less. The concept was intriguing as people want to know what their friends will say about them and are therefore willing to share the Web site. Within a month the site garnered press from every major media outlet, millions of users, and was eventually sold for a hefty sum of money. Some may look at threewords.me's success as a fluke, but from being there firsthand I can tell you it was not. Here is the secret sauce behind threewords.me's success:

- **Zero friction to get started.** A person could get started by typing in her name and registering afterward. It required zero effort to start as a content creator (the person who creates a page requesting feedback). For a content actor (the person who describes the content creator in three words or less) there was also no registration needed. This means that a content creator can get satisfaction out of the system easily and quickly.

- **Social sharing built in.** When setting up a page, a content creator would be asked whether he wanted to get feedback from his friends on Facebook or Twitter. This allowed the content creator to bring a potential mass of thousands of new users into the threewords .me system. There was also an incentive to post a request for their friends to describe them in three words or less, since the people on their Twitter and Facebook lists are most likely the same audience they would want feedback from.

- **A clear double viral loop.** The resounding reason for threewords.me's overnight success is the implementation of a clear double viral loop. Content creators would do all the work by asking their friends to describe them in three words or less. These friends would then become content actors or consumers, but once they interacted with the magic of the service they would soon register to become content creators. Threewords.me is a classic example of a service smoothly transitioning a content actor or content consumer into a content creator.

SEARCH ENGINE OPTIMIZATION

Search engine optimization (SEO) is an older tactic but one that still brings millions of visitors to Web sites. Over the years it's become a dirtier and dirtier area to play in, but when simplified it is an effective and useful technique.

SEO ensures that your Web site and application rank high within search results on various search engines, especially Google. Sure, there are other search engines, but Google is the leader in the market with over 60 percent market share, so as a startup you need to focus your resources on where you can get the most bang for your buck. Most of the other search engines aim to copy Google anyway, which means optimizing for Google will take care of most other search engines.

Search engines work by figuring out what a consumer is searching for based on a few words they type into the engine. The higher you rank in search results, the more likely you are to get traffic from those searches. In the past this was achieved as more and more people visited your site after searching for certain terms. But, sadly, a swarm of consultants and experts who have cropped up over the past decade have manipulated actual results to favor those willing to pay a premium for their services. Fortunately there are still ways to improve your rank without paying a consultant tens of thousands of dollars a month. Here are some of them:

- **Architect your site well.** Search engine optimization is exactly that, optimization. SEO is all about making sure that the content on your Web site is properly optimized for search engines to find and rank it high

THE ULTRALIGHT STARTUP

enough. Make sure that simple details in your code like title tags, keywords, sitemaps, and alternative text for your images are taken care of from Day One. You're more likely to turn up in search results if you use terms that people search for.

- **Write topic-specific content frequently.** Content marketing is a huge way to gain traffic not only by becoming an expert but through SEO. If a piece of content marketing becomes popular enough, it will start to rank for specific terms while increasing the overall value of your site. To do this well you have to produce content frequently.

- **Don't engage in black hat tactics.** Many consulting companies or even startups themselves try to engage in black hat tactics that try to trick Google. These include hiding a long list of keywords or automatically redirecting a user to a more malicious site, such as pornography or gambling, that may be on Google's banned list. Some startups find this beneficial because it allows them to rank high for keywords they don't really rank for or want to include. This might work at first, but the risk of getting banned for foul play isn't worth it. SEO is a hard game but it's worth playing by the rules.

- **Make as much available as possible.** If you are developing an app that has pages with rich and highly searchable content, make sure they are publicly available. LinkedIn took advantage of this by making profile pages highly indexable by search engines. When you search for a person, odds are that their LinkedIn profile comes up as one of the first results. This can also be seen with Wikipedia. When was the last time you searched for something and a Wikipedia entry was not one of the first results on a Google search page?

■ **Match your PR message to your SEO strategy.** Make the message you give in your press strategy match the keywords and phrases you want to rank highly for. The sites of top blogs and newspapers will almost always have higher SEO ranks than your own site. By having your message spread to their site and link back to yours, the ranking starts to trickle down.

Example: About.com

SEO works for all companies but is extremely successful for content-focused companies such as About.com, which was acquired by the *New York Times* in 2005, a year after being valued at over a billion dollars. About.com was successful because it managed to drive 80 percent of its traffic through SEO.

One of the ways it did this was by dividing its content into verticals. Verticals can be thought of as categories or ways to classify content. Some examples might include: auto, health, finance, and fashion. By digging in deep and dividing content this way, About.com was able to approach a large amount of long tail content. (The long tail refers to a large number of terms that get a lot of traffic as a whole but very few on an individual basis.) This SEO strategy lets them win across specific categories.

REFERRAL PROGRAMS

Word-of-mouth marketing has always been one of the most powerful customer acquisition techniques not only in the digital world but in the real world as well. Companies that can effectively incentivize customers to refer others build up a strong customer acquisition channel that would take the competition years to build.

A referral program works to harness existing customers who find your service useful by letting them invite friends into the system. These used to cost tens of thousands of dollars and take a large amount of developer resources to set up. Now, however, in addition to social sharing sites that allow people to refer others, companies such as zferral allow you to set up a referral program for little effort and money.

To incentivize users to sign up, offer some type of reward. There are several that work well:

- **Money.** Money is a strong motivator. If the referees are existing users they will feel great about recommending something they believe in. The fact that money is being used as motivation does not taint the genuine aspect of asking for a referral.
- **Service upgrade.** This is a better option for startups, which may not have a ton of cash. Instead of offering cash, offer users more benefits on the service in exchange for referrals. The rewards that are tied to the service are almost always worth more than their cash equivalent to the user, but still cost less for the company to produce than the cash equivalent .

- **Two-sided referral program.** A two-sided referral program not only rewards the user who helped bring in her friends but also rewards the new users with a bonus. A two-sided referral program makes the same offer available to both sides, so that both are incentivized to participate.

Example: Dropbox

Dropbox is mentioned numerous times throughout this book and for good reason. It has nailed everything from a great product to a great business model, but the key driver to Dropbox's growth has been its referral program. Through this program, Dropbox increased its number of registered users from one hundred thousand to four million in fifteen months (from September 2008 to January 2010), when 35 percent of their daily signups came from their referral program.

Here's how Dropbox's referral program became so successful:

- **They provided a two-sided referral system.** Dropbox incentivized current and new users to participate in the referral system by offering extra storage to each. By incentivizing them with more of the same product they were already paying for, they gave users something no one else could for very little cost.
- **They used an invite-only system.** Dropbox started as an invite-only product, which created a sense of scarcity. The only way to gain access to the Dropbox system was through an invite or a referral from an existing user who shared a folder with you. Existing users usu-

ally shared invitations with people they knew, but there were many times when individuals got invites from complete strangers through the comments section of a blog post. The scarcity of Dropbox invites made the referral system accelerate almost instantly as friends of users would ask to be referred into the system.

- **They built the referral program into the interface.** Dropbox users can share folders with potential users directly from within their computer's file folders. The notification system Dropbox uses also notifies users when a friend they invited joins the shared folder, meaning a referral bonus has been earned. By making the referral program part of the user experience rather than an extra feature, you automatically generate more users.

AFFILIATE PROGRAMS

An affiliate program lets a merchant or service set up a way for others to market their product in exchange for a high cut of revenue from anything they sell. They often cost very little to set up by using software such as zferral, but they take a lot of time to build into a proper channel.

Affiliate programs are not a technology problem but a marketing and relationship problem. Executing on the affiliate program takes the most time and effort as it is an ongoing initiative. The technology stays fairly constant after a first setup, and you have to make sure you have someone (usually in your marketing department) monitoring it carefully as soon as you set it up. This person should promote the affiliate program and make sure affiliates get paid fairly and on time.

Example: Amazon

Amazon has seen a ton of growth through their affiliate program, which is known as Associates. They have nine hundred thousand other Web sites in the program and have generated millions of sales over the years through it. Think of it like this: Amazon's affiliate program has essentially brought them an army of nine hundred thousand salespeople who are only paid on commission. There are three things Amazon did to make their affiliate program the most successful in history:

- **Straightforward rates.** The rates that Amazon paid out to affiliates were straightforward. Affiliates knew how much they would be paid and when on a product-by-product basis. By making your affiliate program straightforward, you can attract better affiliates to promote your program.
- **Diverse list of creative.** Amazon provides not only basic banner ads but intense technology to embed their products into publisher's Web sites. By having diverse creative, affiliates were able to make Amazon products a true part of their site's experience.
- **Easy to integrate for affiliates.** Integration is robust yet easy for affiliates. The affiliate portion of their site works well and lets an "Amazon Associate" get up and running almost instantly. Many affiliate programs require a decently in-depth approval process, which of-

ten turns off potential new affiliates. Amazon, on the other hand, keeps the process simple, letting affiliates get started in absolutely no time.

WEB ADVERTISING

Web advertising can often cost too much for young startups but it is still important to understand how it works. You may eventually find yourself in a position to use it as a customer acquisition technique and will want to be ready to go.

Web advertising works just like any other form of advertising except that it is fully measurable and can be applied at a more detailed level. There are books devoted solely to the topic of making Web advertising perform for your business. This basic primer focuses less on how to apply Web advertising and more on how to make Web advertising cost efficient. First off, it's good to know the three ways that a startup might pay for Web advertising:

- **CPM (cost per impression).** Using this metric you pay a certain small amount for every thousand page views. The higher the quality of the audience, the higher the CPM. Most brand and display advertising (that is, banner ads designed simply to make you aware of a product) uses this metric.
- **CPC (cost per click).** Using this metric you pay on a per-click basis. Every time a user clicks on your ad on the publisher's site you pay the agreed-upon amount. This is primarily how Google makes money on the Internet with AdWords.

- **CPA (cost per action).** With this metric you pay only if a customer pays for your product and you profit. It is the metric most commonly used by affiliate networks.

Example: Zynga

Zynga is one of the largest advertisers on Facebook and accounts for a significant portion of their advertising revenue. The company was able to utilize advertising on Facebook to acquire a large number of new users over time primarily using a mix of CPC and CPM advertising. This multibillion-dollar company knows how much they need to spend for advertising to be worth the cost. They also know that once they acquire a customer they generally have them for life, so the risk of spending money to attract them is small.

IN-PERSON EVENTS

Hosting in-person events is a great way to bring together an audience of customers and community members. These can be done on the cheap and often for free. In a high-tech world, it's often easy to forget about the importance of face time with customers and potential users. You may not be able to reach tens of thousands of people through in-person events the way you can with online marketing, but the quality of such interaction makes up for the quantity.

In-person events allow you to do the following things:

- **Build community.** People who attend these events are often passionate users who will want to spread the word about your product or mission. Even if the event isn't specifically about your product, everyone who attends will know that your startup put on the event. They are also a great way to bring like-minded people together in one room. When two people meet and form a bond, they often remember where it happened. Being the catalyst for that bond will result in those users bringing in other users.

- **Identify leaders.** If you can get people excited about what you're doing, these early evangelists will often become the best vehicles to spread the word about your product. Your startup may help set up the first few events, but ideally you want to facilitate these events so they become self-starting.

- **Become a thought leader.** The best startups help provide utility by educating potential users with new information. People are hungry for knowledge and much more likely to use your product if they can learn something new first. In-person events are a great way to establish yourself as an expert.

- **Gain feedback.** Talking to existing users one-on-one is a great way to gain feedback that can improve your product. Take the time to figure out what features existing customers want to see and what problems they might be experiencing. It may not be a direct way to acquire customers, but learning what other needs your product can serve might be a smart way to acquire customers in the future.

Here's the best way to put on an in-person event for your startup:

- **Pick a topic.** Have a specific topic that you want the event to cover in an educational format. Make sure it is related to your product and is something you can speak to as an authority.
- **Partner with local organizations.** If you're just starting out, it might be hard to attract enough people to your event. Partnering with local organizations such as a coworking space or popular tech meetup group is a good way to increase head count and visibility.
- **Have enough time to execute.** Make sure you have enough time to properly plan your event. The surefire way to make an event fail is not to spend enough time planning it and attracting an audience. Six weeks is usually best. Spend the first two weeks planning and the final four weeks promoting and figuring out the details. After the first few events, this timeframe can be reduced as you will have a strong group of repeat attendees and won't have to work as hard to spread the word.
- **Throw it close to your headquarters.** The first event should be in the same city as your startup. That way your founding team and early employees will be able to attend and you'll be able to draw on your local connections.
- **Provide food and drink.** Serving food gives people an excuse to go to the event and to linger once they're there. To get food on the cheap, think about teaming up with a company that already has money such as Microsoft or a law firm. They get access to the same audience and you save money.
- **Use Meetup and social media.** The easiest place to start

and grow your event is through the Web site Meetup .com. It's a great form of distribution, a good way for new people to find your event, and a pretty standard place to get attendees on board. You should also have the event distributed and promoted through the company's social media channels. It may not bring a large group of attendees, but every extra person counts.

- **Deliver schwag.** Make sure that you are fully stocked with some form of schwag to give away to attendees at the event . The best type of schwag is usually a T-shirt. The T-shirt should have more than just a logo on it and be something catchy to the eye. People love T-shirts, and if they wear them they give your brand visibility to a larger audience.

- **Follow up afterward.** Most startups forget this step, but it's critical to making sure your relationships last. Collect the e-mail addresses of those who register for and attend the event. After the event, be sure to send a quick thank-you note from your own e-mail address and ask for any feedback directly. Don't use a survey as they often take way too much time to fill out.

Example: WordPress and WordCamps

The first WordCamps were organized by Automattic, the company behind WordPress, but now hundreds of WordCamps take place every year across the globe. These conferences, which have no set agenda until they start, are designed to bring together developers and users in the community. Here are the key takeaways from what Automattic did to make WordCamps a resounding success for their company:

- **Takes a hands-off approach.** Automattic selects a specific topic for each WordCamp but does not dictate what happens at the event itself. Instead, the community discusses specific topics and figures out where to go with the event.
- **Provides resources.** Although they leave the running of the event to the community, Automattic does provide resources in the form of promotion and branding to make sure the events do as well as possible for those organizing them.
- **Has a flagship event.** Even though each WordCamp is individually organized, WordCamp in San Francisco is organized by Automattic. It's the flagship event that sets the tone for the rest of the year. By setting up a great event, they bring in participants from across the globe who are often inspired to put together WordCamps themselves.

7

GROWING YOUR STARTUP

THE TACTICS OUTLINED in the previous chapter are great ways to increase your customer count when you're starting out. But as you begin to grow, there are even more efficient ways to develop your business.

THE ART OF BUSINESS DEVELOPMENT

Business development involves partnering with other companies to grow your customer base.

The best startups in the world were able to get where they are today because of early business development. Sure, Google had a lot of insider traction in Silicon Valley when they started, but what made Google really take off was its early business development deals. They were able to cut deals with portals like AOL and power search on Yahoo!. The rest is history.

Let's take a look at how you can master the art of business development and cut deals to make yourself get Google-like early traction.

Going for Wide Distribution

Because your goal is growth, you have to go for wide distribution in your business development deals. When you're starting out, your startup consists only of you and a few other people. It is not humanly possible for you to tackle a large number of deals, so you need to go after larger deals that bring you a lot of distribution. You can't rely on a spray-and-pray approach with business development; you have to target and aim high. Look at how many new customers you're likely to get and the amount of time it will take you to complete a deal. If a deal will take you three times as long as another one but will get you twenty times the amount of customers, go for it. The deal may take longer, but once it goes live it has the potential to make your company.

Don't Work with Assholes

You have to have a "no asshole" policy. I learned about this concept from a good friend of mine, Josh Guttman, the former CEO of Surphace. He says that when negotiating business development deals that could provide wide distribution you need to make sure the people you are trying to partner with are not assholes when it comes to terms, speed, or process. Deals that could provide wide distribution may always seem like they're a week away, but partners who are less than honorable will prolong the process indefinitely.

With Onswipe we were fortunate enough to cut a deal with Automattic that let us power the tablet traffic of 18.6 million sites through WordPress. That gave what we're doing instant credibility and Facebook-level scale. The team at Automattic was great and worked relentlessly with us to get the deal done. We knew they were great people to work with when we observed the following traits:

- They were willing to get the actual deal terms done fast because they believed in the product.
- They took their time putting the product live in order to ensure the best possible outcome for all parties.
- All parties of the company were involved, including the CEO and cofounders.

Try to Set a Standard

It's not always about the money when it comes to cutting a business development deal. As a small startup, you want to gain credibility fast and set a standard. Don't look for partners who simply offer you large sums of money; look for deals that will let you set a standard for what you are doing. Part of that is scale—wide distribution, as mentioned above—but it's also about being the first to market with that scale. If you can set a standard at scale, you will become a market leader overnight.

At Onswipe we cut a deal with the *New York Times* to power their tablet Web traffic advertising. Our platform was simple, elegant, and ready to use. Large companies such as AOL had spent years trying to do the same thing by setting a new advertising standard, but our small startup was able to achieve it in a matter of a few months. We made a little bit of money, but the honest truth is that we would have done it for free. We were able to set the standard for tablet advertising overnight.

Partner with Those Who Share Your Customers

One of my favorite business development tricks is to find a partner who has the same exact customer base as I do but is not competitive at all. Theoretically you could partner with direct competitors to gain wide distribution, but there's no way that will ever fly. At Onswipe, we often work with premium advertising networks to introduce us to their publishing partners. This lets us get in touch with a large number of publishers at once. In return, the advertising networks get a new piece of ad inventory that sells for a very high rate, which makes them more money. Here are some ways to coax such partners into doing a deal with you:

- **Show that there's increased value for their customers.** By showing that their customer will gain more value by partnering with you on their product, they see what's in it for them. Never mention what you get out of the deal.
- **Go to the meetings yourself.** Make sure the CEO and/or founders go to the meeting to get the deal done. Even though you're small, people will appreciate the fact that an executive is coming to the meeting; it signals that you care about the result.
- **Emphasize the opportunity for revenue.** If the deal will actually bring the potential partner revenue, make sure to bring this up as soon as possible. Money talks when you're trying to get deals done. If it is a large-scale partner, they probably get hundreds of inquiries a year. Most of those inquiries don't make them money, so this is a chance to stand out.

▪ **Emphasize the opportunity to look innovative.** This is true in the advertising agency world and many other niches. With Onswipe, tablets are a completely new medium—one that could potentially save the publishing and advertising world. We enable advertisers to create award-winning campaigns with a new medium that will make them look like pioneers. If you can do this, you will play to your partner's ego. If money talks, it's ego that listens.

Who You Should and Shouldn't Talk To

Deals often die when startups try to talk to the wrong people inside an organization. Make sure you know exactly who you want to talk to when you start a conversation about a potential deal. Not spending time with the wrong people is just as important as spending time with the right ones. Here are some good rules to keep in mind when figuring out whom to talk with at an organization:

▪ **Don't spend too much time with the technical team.** These guys will get caught up in technical details and are often difficult to work with. They'll want to suggest a ton of features and try to seem smarter than they are. Try to make this a quick conversation and a simple point of due diligence.

▪ **Don't spend time with the revenue department.** Just because they manage the money doesn't mean they have the authority over how to use it. Talking to the money folks is usually a waste of time.

▪ **Don't spend too much time with the junior person.** You

might have to start with lower-level staff to get you inside the organization but they might not have the clout to move the conversation forward. Try to get them to bring in someone more senior.

- **Do spend time with the decision maker.** Who this is is going to vary depending on the organization and the type of deal, but the person who is in charge of making the final decision needs to get behind your product as soon as possible. It's hard to pick these folks out at first, but they're often the ones who are on every e-mail chain, staying silent until something major is being talked about. You can also ask bluntly: "Who can help make this happen here so we can all win?"

APPLICATION PROGRAMMING INTERFACES

In addition to partnering with other companies, there are several ways to expand your business on your own. One of these ways is to use application programming interfaces (APIs). APIs allow your company to have a more versatile product and therefore gain further reach, by giving others a way to build on your product and make it their own. If you have ever seen Google Maps used on another site, you have seen an API in action. By making the API to Google Maps open, Google has seen wide distribution of its product across the Internet.

At Onswipe, we've opened up our APIs so that anyone can build touch-enabled Web apps and put beautiful advertising with them. They can build their own layouts and extend the functionality of what their publication looks like.

Caterina Fake, the cofounder of Flickr, referred to APIs as "Business Development 2.0." In other words, companies don't need to cut a deal with you to do interesting things with your product; they can easily "do a deal" by taking advantage of the API you offer. As with a great business development deal, APIs allow you to gain traction and market your product in a number of ways:

- **By extending the value of your product to potential customers.** Maybe you don't really care if people build new and exciting products with your startup, but you certainly do want more customers. By having an open API, you let potential customers get more interested in your product since they can customize it to their own needs or mash it up with their existing systems.

- **By getting your product into the hands of many more users.** Many products have grown wildly by having other products extend their functionality for widespread use. Dropbox launched an API and now almost every iPad and iPhone productivity app makes use of a user's Dropbox account. This means that Dropbox is now exposed to every single new user that developers utilizing the Dropbox API bring through the door.

- **By exciting developers.** You will not find a more passionate group of evangelists than a developer community. By providing a great API and platform you ensure that a raging fan base of developers will get on board to promote your product.

Examples: Twitter and Facebook

Twitter built up its user base heavily by having a robust API. The twitter.com Web site has always provided a subpar experience, especially in the early days. By opening up the API, Twitter allowed developers to extend the functionality to a whole new level. A wide range of Twitter clients for iPhone, Android, and BlackBerry were created in order to expand the cross-platform utility of the service. Along with Twitter clients came obvious features such as built-in photo and video sharing. Services like TwitPic have made its founders millions of dollars by providing tons of utility. If it were not for a robust API, Twitter would not have these features, which have become absolutely crucial to the user experience.

Facebook, on the other hand, not only expanded the utility of the site by turning it into a full- fledged platform, but, more important, created an entire new economy. By having a robust platform, social games companies such as Zynga sprouted up inside the Facebook platform. Zynga is now a multibillion-dollar company that could not have grown to the size it is today without the help of Facebook's social infrastructure for their rapid user acquisition.

MOBILE PLATFORMS

Since 2007, mobile platforms have been a huge source of growth for many startups. Some startups are built solely on these platforms, but this conversation concerns startups whose apps on mobile platforms are an auxiliary to their main Web site. With hundreds of millions of devices, mobile platforms are a new way for users to discover your product.

Because of the nature of the Onswipe product, I have had plenty of battles with app stores. To counter the expensive and time-consuming nature of creating apps is just making sure that the tablet version of your product work well in the browser. With HTML5 and JavaScript, you can provide most of the functionality of an app while having it work across all devices.

But certain startups have a legitimate reason to create apps for distribution in mobile app stores. They are usually apps that use deep hardware functionality such as background music, camera recording, and graphics integration. Here's how and why building for mobile platforms can increase distribution for your startup:

- **Task-specific discovery.** People often browse through app stores looking for new functionality and ways to expand the capabilities of their device. Try to target what you are doing to a specific task and identifiable piece of functionality. The purpose of your app should be clearly spelled out in a sentence or two and perform a specific task.

- **Important new functionality.** Mobile app platforms can bring new users into your product if you make new functionality available that takes advantage of the device's capabilities. A mobile app shouldn't just be a replica of what your site can do on the desktop; it should take advantage of features on mobile devices. Apps are really a synonym for "stuff to do" and if you can provide more "stuff to do" with the device, people will be inclined to use your app.

- **Topping the charts.** When it comes to app stores, the fastest way to grow is to top the charts of an app store. This is a lofty goal, but it's achievable if you can find a way to accelerate and maintain your growth.
- **Cross-platform strategy.** The best way to approach mobile devices and apps is by having a cross-platform strategy. Your product cannot work on just one platform or device type, but should work across all device types. This includes iPhone, Android, and, most important, tablet devices. To create the right type of awareness and make use of mobile platforms you just cannot have gaps on other platforms. The problem with doing this right is that it's expensive and time consuming. Focus on the two main platforms with the most distribution, which are iOS and Android at the moment.

Example: Pandora

Pandora, a popular music streaming service, is the best example of a company that extended its reach and exponentially increased its growth using mobile platforms. Taking advantage of the platform provided by the iPhone after it was released, Pandora almost doubled its size overnight. Here's how they did it:

- **Made to be mobile.** Music is meant to live on the go, not just be tethered to your desk. With its service, Pandora leveraged a specific pain point—namely that you needed a computer to use it—that only mobile could solve. Pandora was already quite popular, but their mobile strategy helped them grow.

- **First mover on new features.** The one feature everyone longed for Pandora to have was background audio streaming, but this was prevented by Apple until 2010. Background audio streaming lets a user listen to music even when they leave the Pandora app to work on another task, like sending a tweet or browsing the Web. Pandora knew this and became the first mover to take advantage of the feature. Even copycat competitors took months to match Pandora's functionality on this.

- **A multiperson experience.** Pandora is used individually but also in groups, power music at parties or in the car when you're driving with friends. When building out your mobile app and thinking how it can be used to get new customers involved, make sure you build the experience to involve more than just one person. Pandora facilitated the social nature of its product by allowing users to share their music library with other users on a different device.

Now that we've covered various strategies for acquiring customers, it's time to figure out how to get them to pay you for your product.

8

HOW TO MAKE MONEY

I HOPE YOU'RE having a lot of fun running your startup and building a product you really want to share with the world. But you still need to make money along the way.

Even if you're still in the planning stages and won't be collecting revenue for a while, you still need to consider how you're going to monetize your product. This chapter guides you through all the different business models and successful examples of their use.

FREEMIUM

Venture capitalist Fred Wilson coined the term freemium in mid-2006 and it kicked off a revolution in the Internet industry. Wilson recognized the need for the term when he noticed the ever-increasing number of startups that, having begun by giving their services away for free, realized they could charge for their offerings.

Freemium works by offering multiple tiers of your service.

The first is a basic, free model that allows new customers to try it out and hopefully get hooked. From there you can start charging for more advanced services, attracting revenue from your most loyal users and from power users who want more. Freemium is best applied to software businesses or consumer businesses that have a high level of utility. To set up a freemium service you must first outline the different features of each level of service and showcase them up front so that customers know what to expect and aren't surprised by a sudden paywall or limit. It's best to set rates based on usage, not time, as it gives users control over how much they pay instead of threatening them with an expiration date.

Example: Dropbox

Dropbox has grown to be worth hundreds of millions of dollars largely as a result of its successful execution of the freemium model.

Dropbox offers a small amount (two gigabytes) of storage for free to anyone who signs up. This is enough to get a user hooked on the service but not enough to accommodate all their future needs. When a user uploads past two gigabytes, Dropbox gives them an option to upgrade to more storage space for a fee. At this point the user is probably already relying on the service and will be willing to pay a small amount to continue using it.

But instead of offering paid and unpaid options, Dropbox tiers their pricing to make sure users only pay for the amount of storage they use—whether it is fifty gigabytes or one hundred gigabytes.

Finally, although Dropbox charges a monthly fee, it gives

users the option of paying for the entire year up front at a discount. This way, even if a customer chooses to leave, the company has already guaranteed a certain amount of revenue.

RECURRING SUBSCRIPTION

Recurring subscription models could be a subset of freemiums, but are actually quite distinct. As we've seen, SaaS is software delivered over the Internet instead of being downloaded. This setup lets software companies charge for some metric, usually per user on a monthly basis. This makes the software a variable expense for the user as it scales with the number of users on a noncommittal monthly basis.

To understand how SaaS works, think of a company like Netflix, especially their streaming service. Users pay a certain amount per month, which can be tiered depending on how much they use the service. A user will often sign up for the service, sometimes with a free trial denoted by time, and then pay a monthly fee based on a certain metric or metrics. That monthly fee should rise if the metric rises. Although the idea is similar to a freemium, SaaS differs in that it usually does not provide a free plan, but rather a time-limited free trial. It also usually scales based on the number of individuals using the product, hence making the ceiling of what a developer can charge a customer much higher than with a freemium. In general SaaS is used more by businesses than individual consumers.

Example: Salesforce

Salesforce is considered the pioneer of the SaaS model. The company started over a decade ago and has become the poster child for a software-free world. CEO Marc Benioff has even written a book about the company's mission to bring an end to downloadable software and support the Cloud.

The company started with the simple notion that by making business software such as customer relationship management (CRM) available on the Internet, they could charge for it based on usage. Instead of paying all the money up front (like companies do when purchasing software packages from developers), a company could add a user to the account when needed, transforming software to a variable cost.

The real lesson from Salesforce is that they were able to build a service that works for a team of five or a team of five thousand. With an SaaS business model you allow your offering to scale its revenue across all different customer sizes.

THE APP MODEL

In January 2007, Apple introduced the iPhone to the world. In 2008, the entire software industry was changed with the introduction of the Apple App Store. This signaled a radical change in the way mobile applications were distributed to end users. Before this, distribution required a large deal with a carrier and a poor revenue share that only gave a company a small percentage of profits. Since then, billions of dollars have been paid to app developers.

The app model is similar to the way the software industry

first started decades ago. A user finds something they need or enjoy and pays a one-time fee to use it for as long as they want. Apple and other app stores often take a cut of about 30 percent, which takes care of payment processing, logistics, and data transfer, among other things. All you have to worry about as a developer is getting a check every month.

Pricing in the app world is a tricky subject. It's a mix of looking at what others in the market charge and picking through overall data. Some wildly profitable apps are free and make money through advertising. We'll cover that later on in this chapter.

I mentioned apps in the previous chapter too, but the key difference here is that when your primary application resides in the app store, then the app store is your business model. If the app is an extension of your current Web site or brand, then the app store is a customer acquisition method.

Example: Angry Birds

Angry Birds has been declared by some as the Pac-Man for the twenty-first century. It's a simple little game that has taken the world by storm and would not have been possible without app stores from Apple, Google, and others. Their business model is simple: Develop a game and charge 99¢ for it. Why 99¢? Because the low price point makes Angry Birds an impulse buy for many, and makes Angry Birds much more attractive than more expensive games priced at $4.99 or $9.99. Once popularity rose, the social proof of all the press and their friends playing the game made it a no-brainer for everyone to spend the 99¢.

CONTENT PAYWALLS

The business of paying for content seems to be dying by the second, but if executed well it can be very lucrative. Everyone consumes content in some way, and even though the media through which people do so is changing, the interest in great content is alive and well. If you can make content that people find valuable and will pay for, you are on track to creating a monster business.

The best way for a new business to charge for content is with a paywall. This allows you to showcase some of your content for free but charge a premium for extra or enhanced content. Some paywalls may require a full-blown monthly subscription while some may charge a one-time fee for something such as a research report or a single article. The way to decide how to charge is by looking at whether the value is recurring or is for a simple one-time transaction. You can figure this out by asking frequent users—those who have been on for at least six months—the following questions:

1. How often do you visit the site?
2. Would you have paid for an article the first time you visited the site?
3. Would you now pay for access to that content?

Example: The *New York Times*

The *New York Times* may be an extreme example owing to its size and long reputation, but it's also the best case to scrutinize. In 2010 the paper put together a paywall for all its digital content, but it did not automatically restrict users. Though the *New York Times* is not a startup by any stretch of the imagination, it is a shining example of great content that people are willing to pay for. It applied the following strategy, and you can too on a much smaller scale:

- Not all content was put behind a paywall. Some articles were left for free indefinitely.
- Every reader was allowed to view twenty articles for free before having to pay. This smacks of the freemium model.

The *New York Times* has built a very old brand that has given them credibility and the trust of readers. You may not have as long behind you, but you can certainly build a quality brand that people trust.

MICROPAYMENTS

Micropayments are a new phenomenon that has sprung up over the past decade, mostly resulting from social gaming and the virtual currency market.

Micropayments are usually used to upgrade an experience or to buy a virtual good online. Rarely will a micropayment correlate to something in the real world. PayPal defines micropayments as any amount under $12. In today's world, I would say some amount under $5 is more appropriate, with somewhere less than $1.50 being the perfect representation. Sure, there are things that may cost under $5 in the real world, but the bang for the buck is not the same since the cost to produce an additional copy of a virtual product is essentially zero.

Micropayments are a great way to incorporate game mechanics into the product or the ability to cheat the system. Game mechanics online usually require a user to complete a certain number of tasks to advance to the next level. With micropayments, a user can skip the requirements by paying a small amount for the ability to advance or to get what he needs to advance. If you can integrate the payment process into the actual user experience, these small purchases turn into impulse buys because users will want to continue playing.

Example: FarmVille

FarmVille is a part of the Zynga gaming empire and has turned into a multibillion-dollar sensation in a few short years. The real driver of FarmVille's revenue success comes in the form of credits that users can buy to advance to the next level. They can advance without spending money by completing a series of simple tasks, but many people are willing to shell out a small fee in order to get to the next level quickly. Users can also customize their experience by paying for gifts or decorations. In either case, the choice to pay is controlled by the user.

The formula for successful micropayments like FarmVille is simple: Create desire and allow users to attain it immediately—for just a few bucks.

COMMISSION PAYMENTS

Everyone is always looking for more business, which means there is a lot of money to be made by those who can facilitate the process. If your company specializes in partnering with other businesses as an affiliate or lead generator, you'll probably benefit most from a commission-based payment plan. Businesses are more than happy to pay you a cut of revenue if you can help them sell more, and if you become an expert in a certain market you'll only increase your value.

Example: Hipmunk

Hipmunk set out to tackle a very simple problem that pretty much everyone has to deal with—the high cost and inconvenience of flying. They realized that there was a tremendous amount of pain in searching for and buying flights, so Hipmunk fixed the problem by providing a better experience and more information for those trying to find flights. In exchange, airlines pay them a fee for every ticket purchased using their service. The best way to summarize the Hipmunk model and all successful lead generation is: Better experience + ability to discern information = purchase.

ADVERTISING

Advertising is the business model that makes the Internet world go round. It is how Google, Yahoo!, Facebook, and many others have made their fortunes. Above all other business models, it is the most lucrative, but also the most difficult to execute.

Advertising is pretty straightforward. An application or site creates a compelling audience that brands and companies want to reach. In order to reach that audience, companies pay for advertising on that app or site. The key benefits behind advertising on the Internet over traditional media are:

Targeting. Your company is able to target a very specific audience with the data they have on users, therefore advertisers can create ads based upon interests and characteristics of people on the site.

Accountability. In the traditional media world, advertising has always been a guessing game because advertisers could never gauge exactly how many customers they gained from ads. Online advertising allows them to collect real data on how many people saw their ad and were directed to purchase because of it.

Example: Facebook

Facebook is currently worth tens of billions of dollars on the private market and for good reason. They not only have a massive audience but a massive amount of data that makes that audience infinitely more valuable.

Another valuable asset of Facebook is its ability to create advertising very easily. In under fuve minutes I can create an ad that targets male students at New York University with an interest in politics. All successful companies with an advertising business model follow their self-serve approach in which advertisers sign up on their own and start using the system immediately.

SUPPORT

Even the best interfaces and products encounter users who aren't savvy, and even those who are savvy will want to have someone hold their hand along the way. Support and professional services are a huge revenue model for software startups that don't want to charge for their product.

Support works best for startups in the open source world, where software is available for free, but often comes "as is," meaning the user doesn't benefit from things like installation help, troubleshooting, or frequent updates.

Companies offering support systems simply charge a customer for advanced support along with professional services such as training and installation. The support business model requires a company to have human capital that can handle support requests as they come in. It does not scale as easily as digital business models such as advertising or micropayments.

Example: SugarCRM

SugarCRM is a leading provider of customer relationship management software, but instead of selling the software for a fixed price per month like Salesforce, they give it away for free as an open source download. Though the software is free to download and use, many businesses gladly pay Sugar an exorbitant amount of money for support and professional services.

The best tactic to convert free customers into paying customers is to make the software ask for an e-mail address and a small amount of company information upon download. Those most likely to pay for support and professional services are larger companies with the capital to do so.

APIS AND ACCESS TO DATA

Data runs the world today. Wall Street is a systematic set of robots making trades based upon data, Google delivers tens of billions of dollars of ads a year based upon data, and Facebook knows everything about you. Some companies keep the data for internal use, while others make a whole business out of providing access to data through an application programming interface. As mentioned in Chapter Seven, an API lets a startup use the services of a larger company or startup easily.

Companies will mine data and other sources to provide a robust solution that would be way too difficult for a young company or even a large company to do on its own. This data can vastly improve another company's application and reduce costs, therefore proving its value. It's essentially what non-Internet companies such as InfoUSA have traditionally done: Gather data, synthesize it, and make it universally accessible.

Example: SimpleGeo

SimpleGeo is a startup staffed by an all-star team of executives from Digg and Socialthing! When geolocation applications started to take off, Simplegeo realized that marketers were willing to pay a premium for geolocation data that could help them target customers. Most companies, if not all, do not have the resources to build a strong geolocational database. SimpleGeo made this incredibly simple by developing an API and charging a flat fee every time the API is used one thousand times.

HOW TO KNOW WHAT TO CHARGE

Pricing for your product is not an arbitrary number that comes out of thin air. The companies with the best pricing—those that charge as much as possible without driving away customers—have spent a considerable amount of time testing the pricing of their product. Figuring out your business model(s) is only the first step, as pricing determines how receptive a large base of your customers are.

A/B Test Pricing with Customers

The easiest way to see what pricing resonates with your customers is to A/B test your entire pricing scheme. A/B testing refers to using one variable, the A variable, and testing another, the B variable. The A variable and B variable are on the same metric or plane, such as price or a line of copy, but will each have a different value. For example, the A variable will be $5 a month and the B variable $10 a month. The A variable could also be something as simple as one line of text while the B variable could be more complex, multiple phrases of copy. But the most powerful variable to test is price, to determine how sensitive potential customers are to your pricing plans. Variables let you present different choices to users and the one that more users choose is the one you should end up using permanently. This is a fine line as you want to make sure it is not price discrimination. The goal is to show slightly different pricing, pricing models, and value propositions to your potential customers. Here are some tips on what to test and how to test:

- Keep the same number of general pricing plans or options. For example, if you're testing a freemium, keep the three tiered levels of pricing you have always been charging for.
- Change the pricing of the different service levels on a month-to-month basis. If the pricing reads $25, $50, and $100 for the three different plans, then you should A/B test at a range around $35, $60, and $125 per month in the next cycle.
- Start highlighting different plans more to see if changing the price increases the conversion of one plan over the other.
- Modify the benefits associated with each plan. For example, if you're Dropbox and your basic plan at $25 only gives access to a certain amount of storage, test to see if conversion is affected if you double this amount.

To get started with A/B testing use a tool called Optimizely, which automates the entire A/B test process by specifying the exact A and B variables you would like to test. It's affordable, works for companies of all sizes, and has an easy-to-use interface.

Setting Different Tiers

Set up different tiers with some prices much higher than others. By doing this you can see how a small subset of users are sensitive to other forms of pricing. It's also a great way to funnel people into the pricing that you want.

Some companies will tier pricing in a way that highlights the middle of the road and displays it prominently. A company may know its best price but want to make the other plans seem too expensive on the high end and not that capable on the low end.

Give It All Away for Free to Beta Testers

The best way to know what to charge is to have a large enough dataset to analyze. In order to get this size dataset, give the service away for free to as many people as possible for a short period of time. It may cost a decent amount of capital, but in return you are given access to data. From this data you can see where people engage, what features people don't use, and even what features people want in the future.

A potential huge pitfall of giving away your product for free to beta testers is the failure to communicate throughout the testing process. If you are giving your service away for free and planning to charge later on, then you will have to communicate with your community along the way. You do not want to seem as if you are pulling a bait and switch. Make sure your users know the service will not be free forever.

Equate Tier Increases to Quantifiable Benefits

The best way to charge is to equate increases in price with quantifiable benefits that a user will be able to understand. It's not about features, but benefits. Here are some of the quantifiable benefits that might mean something to a user:

Storage. Show a user that they can increase their storage on your service, but tell them what that equates to in terms of what they are storing. When Apple introduced the first iPod they often quoted the amount of music five gigabytes of storage would hold. They referred to it as thousands of songs in your pocket, not gigabytes of songs in your pocket.

Personalization. Everyone loves to make something on their own and they will often pay for the privilege of doing so. Examples include custom premium theme selections or the ability to use a custom domain. In the business-to-business world, companies will often pay more to remove the branding of your service and have the product look as if it is their own.

Security. People often pay for comfort and ease of mind. You can start to include levels of security functionality in certain pricing tiers. You can also put in redundancy and backups as another way to coax customers to upgrade their plans.

Support. Most people get lost in products or just want a safety net. That safety net usually comes in the form of support. Users on the consumer end will pay more for company support rather than wide-open forums. On the business end, companies will pay for faster response time. If people are relying on your software for critical functionality, they will often pay more for access to faster support.

Removal of advertising. Most users hate Web advertising. Ads are often ugly, intrusive, and bring down the user experience. Instead of supporting the site by viewing ads they ignore, users will often be open to paying for the removal of ads on a premium account.

Mobile device access. Some services do not allow access to mobile apps and Web sites on free or cheaper plans. You can give mobile access as an exclusive feature to customers who pay more. Individuals who want mobile access are most likely power users and cannot live without your service.

Looking at Competitors

One of the best ways to set pricing tiers in the beginning is to price your product at or below the price of your competitors. Your competitors most likely have spent a lot of time, money, and effort figuring out what to charge. Odds are they have also validated that pricing with their customers over time, otherwise they wouldn't be pricing that way. Here are the questions you should ask yourself when looking at a competitor's pricing scheme:

- How many tiers do they have?
- What do they give away for free?

- What do they charge for?
- What are the metrics and basis for their pricing?
- How much do they charge?
- When did they change their pricing?

Avoid a Race to the Bottom

The biggest problem in any industry occurs when companies compete solely on price and end up in a race to the bottom. Although you should pay attention to a competitor's pricing, you should use it only as a guideline, not a rule. Don't be reactive in pricing and go for the gas station effect. Most gas stations are placed right across the street from each other and change their pricing when their competitor does in order not to lose business. The difference is that gasoline is a commodity and doesn't change from station to station. You don't want to undermine the value of your product by riding on the fact that it's the cheapest. Here's what you should emphasize in order to make sure you don't start a race to the bottom with your pricing:

Interface and design. This is why people pay way more for the beauty of Apple products over boring PC equivalents. Make the best products possible with beautiful design and people will pay you more.

Support and customer love. Zappos ended up beating other shoe retailers not because they were any better at selling shoes but because they knew how to sell a great customer experience.

Compatibility. Many companies use different pieces of software, such as CRMs, project management apps, and blogging tools. If you can fit in to their existing workflow of products, that helps immensely.

Difference in what you pay for. You can compete directly with another company by charging for a different element of the product than they charge for. If a competitor charges based on the number of users, try charging based on the amount of storage space instead.

9

MAKE YOUR STARTUP FAMOUS

MEDIA ATTENTION IS key not only to the original success of a startup, but to its continued success as well. We live in a noisy world in which every company is vying to get noticed by the press, and the days when this could be done by firing off a press release to some national outlets are long over. Luckily, despite the competition for attention, you don't need a lot of money—just a lot of creativity—to get noticed.

HOW TO GET NOTICED BEFORE YOU LAUNCH

In order to make a splash when you finally launch, you need to start causing a ruckus and getting the attention of others way beforehand. By creating anticipation, you build an audience of people excited about your product. They will no doubt pay attention when you finally release it to the world. Here are a few simple ways to do this:

Collect E-mails from Day One

E-mails are the lifeblood of any prelaunch startup–even more important than Twitter followers or Facebook Likes. Make sure your startup's landing page includes a way for people to give you their e-mail address and entice them to do so by offering something like early access to the product when it's ready. This gives you a direct line to those most interested in your product early on.

Pick Fights with People Bigger Than You

People love a good David and Goliath story, so don't be afraid to pick fights with industry leaders and huge companies to gain attention. This will raise your profile by putting you on an equal footing with those way out of your league. Of course you want to be respectful, but do not be afraid to be bold. The media loves stories about the smaller startup that is willing to take on the large corporate giant.

One of my proudest moments was when I called out Rupert Murdoch, the billionaire media mogul, in the press. It was well before we launched Onswipe, but people were excited about what we were building. His new pet project, *The Daily*, was a horrid failure and I had a few suggestions on how to make it better—namely by employing the same tools I was already using at Onswipe. My suggestions included having better tablet-focused design and making the content Web-based instead of downloadable. I coordinated with a press outlet, *Wired*, letting them read the post early so they could write an article that linked back to it. It was a symphony of press beauty. My post would come online thirty minutes before the *Wired* article was published. The response was great and let us establish ourselves as a legitimate player in the technology space. We received attention from other, smaller bloggers and had an influx of invite requests. Most companies with only a few people do not get put on the same plane as a decades-old media conglomerate such as News Corp.

Blog Early, Blog Often

As soon as you come up with the idea for your startup, start blogging. This may seem obvious now, but too many companies don't put good content out there. If Andres and I hadn't already been blogging we never would have been able to pull off our partnership with *Wired*. It was through our blog that we were able to build an audience and have a voice that would let us call out *The Daily*. Blogging also lets you establish yourself as a thought leader, which in turn allows you to talk about the problem you are solving. This can increase the amount of people who link to you, thereby improving your search traffic.

Be Open About What You're Doing

So many companies think it's cool to be stealthy and not talk about what they're doing. Maybe they're afraid people will steal their ideas or some other nonsense like that, but if you don't talk about what you're doing no one has any reason to pay attention to you. All press is good press—especially early on—and the earlier you can start grabbing mindshare, the better. If you are secretive, no one will write about you. How could they? There's nothing to write about!

Be Mysterious

To clarify the point above, there is a difference between being open and telling the world all your plans. It's good to give the general gist of what you are doing, but you need to leave the audience wanting more. Stealth gives people a reason to ignore you; mystery gives them something to talk about before you launch the company.

The best way to build mystery is to give teasers as you build the product. They could consist of a simple design mockup, a feature, or even a full product video. If you do a full product video, keep it short and highlight key features.

The best way to keep people interested in your teasers is to put them out on a regular schedule, say once a week. Bungie, the company behind the smash hit video game Halo, does this fantastically well. They give weekly Friday updates in which they talk about everything going on, but will usually give insights into what's next on their blog. To get fans excited, they show off new levels from a forthcoming game, one-by-one every week. Die-hard Halo fans and concerned media folks wait around their computers every Friday afternoon, eager to see what will come next. As a result, when Bungie launches a new version or product, everyone knows right away and word spreads quickly.

HOW TO PITCH THE PRESS

There are many ways to draw attention to yourself, but the best way to spread a message with legitimate attention is through the press. Pitching the press is an art. Every startup, established company, and whackadoo in between is vying to get attention, and the best media outlets receive thousands of pitches a day from companies begging to be written about. Determining the best media outlet depends on who you are trying to reach and why. If you're looking for mass appeal you should approach large publications like *Wired* and the *New York Times*. If you're trying to get influential coverage you should approach tech blogs like *TechCrunch*. If you're trying to reach influencers within your industry, you should contact thought leaders in that industry. Getting attention from them is like getting accepted into Harvard—it's hard and it probably won't happen if you don't stand out. So how do you get through the noise and land your product launch on a major media outlet?

Tell a Story

The way the press works is very simple. Most press outlets, whether print or digital, are fueled by advertising. More advertising can be sold if there are more page views. What drives more page views? Great stories. Writers are constantly on the hunt for stories to tell their audience, and if you can give them a good one they'll be much more likely to work with you. You also have to craft what you are doing as something valuable to their audience.

Another key point is utility. If you are a great utility and solve a universal problem for the publication, they will want to write about you.

Solve a Pain Point

When Dropbox launched they were covered with fervor by every press outlet imaginable, especially in the digital space. Here was a tool that made online backup effortless and everyone recognized that the service was immensely useful. The press outlets that covered the launch are now ingrained in the heads of their readers as the place they found out about that awesome utility, Dropbox. Dropbox addressed a simple pain point: "Accessing your files from multiple computers and having them backed up is a pain. We make that easy."

Get to the Point

Never write a long pitch. Instead, craft a great e-mail subject line that suggests the writer is getting an exclusive on a great story their readers will love. Our subject line when we launched PadPressed (which later became Onswipe) was: "Exclusive for TC: Launching Padpressed. Make any blog feel like a native iPad app." Don't write for the journalist; write for the readers. If you can craft a pitch that a normal person will understand, the press outlet will be more likely to cover it. Give them sound bites they can republish or quote. Remember, they receive thousands of pitches a day. They don't have hours upon hours to go through paragraphs of rambling.

Provide Access to Extended Information

Although you always want to get to the point as soon as possible, you also need to provide a way for the writer to get access to more information so they don't ever have to speak to you again. Here is some of the information you should provide:

- **Pictures and videos.** A demo video will do wonders in an article because it gives readers a great idea of what you're doing. Pictures are a must. Most online writers will want to put screenshots or some type of product photo in the article, but they won't want to take the time to find these themselves. And even if they do, you want to control what the reader sees, so it's best to offer them something up front.
- **Feature overviews.** Highlight the key features of the product, the ones that make it unique and appealing. Put a bullet point before each feature and one sentence after it. Don't go wild here; keep it to five features or fewer.
- **Basic company information.** This should include the names of the founders and where you're based. Also include funding details and any other useful background information.
- **The significance of what's being announced.** Tell them what is new about what you are announcing and why it's worth writing about. This should reinforce the hook of the story.

Be Available

News travels fast. After you pitch an outlet, make sure to be fully available for the rest of the day to answer any questions a writer may have. Your ability to answer important questions can determine whether a story gets published. If you are missing in action, the writer will just move on to the next story. I usually give a writer my Skype username, cell phone number, and e-mail address in all initial communications.

Piggyback on Other Stories

There is always a hot trend or story of the moment, especially in the tech world. Writers love to stick to these trends because they know readers will be interested and because it allows them to position the outlet as a go-to source of valuable information. It follows that any company that is part of the trend in some way will get a lot of attention. The problem with trends is that everyone is talking about them, so it's hard to make yourself heard. If you find a way to add some exclusive new insight into the trend, then journalists will be more likely to write about you.

One of my first products, the one I developed when I was nineteen, was a marketplace for college kids akin to eBay. Looking back, I see it was a horrible idea that had been tried by many people before me, but somehow I was still able to get a tremendous amount of press coverage. Why? I released the product in early 2005, at the same time eBay was hiking fees for sellers, so I was able to take advantage of all the coverage of eBay and pitch my product as a great alternative for students to save money. I got picked up by the Associated Press, which allowed the story to reach every major media outlet imaginable, including *USA Today*.

Deliver the Message Yourself

PR firms tend to annoy writers a lot, as they interrupt them or don't add a personal touch to a story. The best PR firms have built up relationships over time with most writers, but odds are you can't afford them. In fact, you may not be able to afford any PR firm. This is fine, though, because when you're starting out no one can convey passion and excitement for your startup quite like you can. Writers pick up on this and it motivates them to write about you. Also, the fact that you took the time to reach out to them directly means a lot.

Give an Exclusive

This one is tricky, and it can backfire if you do it wrong. If there is a major announcement coming, reach out to a top press outlet and give them a twenty-four- to thirty-six-hour exclusive on what you're announcing. This will make them more likely to write about it, but it may also put other writers off. At the end of the day, though, it's sometimes worth it to bruise a few egos to get the best outlet you can for your story. Rotate launch event exclusives across different outlets to keep everyone happy.

Help the Writer Out

When a writer is waffling over whether to run a story because it does not seem interesting, I usually ask them, "What can I do to make this a great story for you?" They don't want generic press release rewrites, but something that can benefit them. Take the time to figure out how you can personalize the story for their audience. With Onswipe, we approached the education writer from ReadWriteWeb after our first round of funding. The funding story was old but what we were up to was not. We ended up crafting an interesting story around our take on how Onswipe could be applied to the education market.

Give Something Away

Giveaways are a great incentive for the media, especially if they come in the form of early invites or trials of a service. This gives the outlet the opportunity to offer their audience access to something they can't get elsewhere. Once again, it's all about letting a writer add value for their audience. Here are some suggestions on doing a successful giveaway:

- **Limit the number of giveaways.** This creates scarcity so more people will take advantage of it right away. Just make sure you say up front that the offer is limited, otherwise people will get angry if they miss out.
- **Make it go viral.** Require readers to tweet the story or share it on Facebook in order to be eligible. This way the story spreads. It is also useful because it gives the writer of the story more page views.

THE PITCH THAT STARTED IT ALL

When Andres and I were about to launch PadPressed (which later became Onswipe), we decided to pitch the story to

TechCrunch in order to get the traffic rolling. Since *TechCrunch* is the leading tech blog in the world, we knew getting covered by them would give us clout and a lot of attention. The e-mail below, which we sent to Michael Arrington, the founder and editor in chief of *TechCrunch,* is heavily responsible for much of the success that Onswipe has had so far.

Subject: Exclusive for TC: Launching Padpressed.- make any blog feel like a native iPad app

Hey Mike,

Launching PadPressed tomorrow at noon EST and TC gets free rein on an exclusive before then. PadPressed makes any blog look and behave like a native iPad app. We're talking accelerometer aware column resizing, swipe to advance articles, touch navigation, home screen icon support, and more. We've built some pretty cool tech to make this happen smoothly, and it works with your existing layout (iPad layout only activated when the blog is accessed from an iPad). Okay, I'll shut up now and you can check out the demo links/feature pages below, which are much more interesting than my pitch.

P.S. Would also be happy to do giveaways to TC readers. Thanks again and feel free to reach out if you have anymore questions (skype, phone, etc. listed below).

Video Demo: http://vimeo.com/13487300

Live demo site (if you're on an iPad): jasonlbaptiste .com

Feature overviews: http://padpressed.com/features

My contact info: j@jasonlbaptiste.com, Phone: 772.801.1058, Twitter: @jasonlbaptiste, Skype: jasonlbaptiste

-jlb

772.801.1058

You Should Check Out
JasonLBaptiste.com

Notice that "exclusive" is in the subject line and the first sentence of the e-mail. We made it clear this was a hot piece of information and that we were giving it to *TechCrunch* first. We kindly put a deadline on it so they could act quickly enough, but as a rule you don't want to put too early a deadline as writers may be working on other stories.

We made it clear what PadPressed did: Make your blog feel like a native iPad app. The iPad was all the rage (still is) and the app economy was big. Notice that we were riding two trends. More important, we said (and still say), screw the app trend. That's pretty neat stuff and something we knew the *TechCrunch* audience would enjoy.

We also kept the e-mail short and sweet because we knew how stressful it is to wade through long e-mails. We even said as much: I'll shut up. Check it out for yourself.

You'll also notice that we gave Mike every possible way to contact me. This was a really smart move on my part. After one e-mail exchange I received a call. If I did not give my phone number and make myself easily accessible this article might never have happened. Don't do a press launch when you are preoccupied or won't be around to talk. If it is launch time, clear your schedule!

WHEN DISASTER STRIKES

You might assume you don't need to worry about disaster striking early on, but the reality is that most startups are prone to making bad mistakes, and even a little bad press can go a long way. In a world where anyone can complain via Twitter, startups should be ready for the worst and know how to handle it. Not all PR is good PR. If you become successful enough the press will write about your darkest days as well as your brightest. A great startup knows how to handle PR in the worst of times as well as in the best of times. It's also key for a startup founder to develop a thick skin.

Ignore the Trolls

Some people will hate what you're doing just because they want to; there may be absolutely no rhyme or reason behind it. In the online world, these people are known as "trolls." They exist solely to get a rise out of you by provoking you with outlandish comments. Never, ever respond to them. Just keep on going.

Keep a Consistent Stream of Updates

When something goes wrong, you need to keep a constant stream of updates going out to your users and community. Even if problems are minor, the fact that someone is communicating is absolutely huge. No news is bad news in this industry.

Web hosting provider Media Temple is great at this. Whenever something happens that impacts their service, they provide updates throughout the day on their blog and their Twitter account.

Admit When You Have Screwed Up

The best companies admit to their users when they have screwed up royally. You can't always make the best decisions or see what might happen in advance. We live in a world where transparency and authenticity is key. Companies that leverage this can turn a bad situation into a good one.

Chargify, a company that provides subscription billing software, created a huge uproar when they removed an option for a free plan for developers. When the dust settled, the CEO made a promise, apologized, and fixed what had gone wrong.

See their damage control at http://chargify.com/blog/our-promise-and-the-new-launch-plan-pricing-option/.

Waiting Out the Storm

Sometimes change is a very difficult thing and will upset a lot of people. When your startup becomes large enough, there's often no way to avoid this. If the change you are making is part of a key service and strategy initiative in your plans for the long term, you have to wait out the storm. As a CEO, you have to have conviction about what you do.

One of the best examples over the past decade comes from the Facebook News Feed rollout. In 2006, when the company introduced the News Feed—a service that showed a user what all their friends were up to—Facebook was relatively small in comparison to the six hundred million-plus users it now has. The News Feed freaked out many users, causing concerns about privacy and real panic. It was such a radical change that users revolted en masse. Within 24 hours groups were formed and attracted hundreds of thousands of users protesting the change. There was national news coverage. But at the end of the day, Mark Zuckerberg didn't waiver. Facebook knew the importance of the News Feed and that their user base would calm down over time. To this day, the News Feed is the most important invention that Facebook has implemented. Throughout the process, Facebook communicated directly with its users, and Mark Zuckerberg wrote a famous blog post addressing the issue and detailing the steps Facebook would take moving forward.

HOW APPLE KEEPS BUZZ GOING

As I talked about earlier in the chapter, you need to start building buzz well before you launch, but that does not mean you should stop once you're on the market. You need to be able to keep buzz going or you will become irrelevant.

Apple is the master of getting press and building buzz. No company in the world can match what they are able to do. Their process is not only fascinating, but it has been used for over a decade and has yet to fail. The great thing about it is that it is a repeatable process we can analyze for our own benefit. Below are a list of strategies Apple uses to build buzz, some of which we've already talked about:

They're Mysterious

Apple is great at creating a culture of mystery that intrigues observers and stirs up rumors about what's coming next. The company doesn't have to leak things or give teasers since they have created an entire industry dedicated to doing this. Since you are much smaller than Apple, it doesn't hurt for you to give teasers along the way that give a glimpse into what your startup is up to, yet retain your mystery.

They Have a Tweetable Theme

Every Apple launch has a theme that is short and simple enough to be tweeted by anyone, so it spreads throughout the social media ecosystem and the press quickly. The theme sums up what the event or the product is about. When the iPhone was introduced, Apple used the theme "Apple reinvents the phone." It was simple, exciting, and got the message across.

They Highlight More Than Just Apple

At every Apple press event and launch and in every commercial Apple focuses on more than just themselves. The entire "Think Different" campaign was dedicated to highlighting people who would have used the Mac if they were still alive, people like Einstein. The current iPhone commercials feature app developers who have made the device a success over the years. Highlighting the success of others who use your platform is viral in nature. People you spotlight will in return go to their audience to champion what you are doing.

They Have a Predictable Release Cycle

Apple launches its products at a predictable time every year: iPods in the fall, iPhones in the summer, and iPads in late winter. This is great for the consumer but it's also wonderful for the press, who are now in line with Apple's schedule. Apple knows when to start rumors, when to dig through production cycles, and everything in between. Here's what a coinciding hype and release cycle should look like:

- Start building up hype at the end of your most recent release for what might be next. Usually there will be glaring gaps in a product that will let users know what's coming.
- Start talking about the coming features and giving them general timeframes way in advance. Make sure the timeframes are realistic.
- Start leaking screenshots, videos, and early sneak peeks of the product. You can do this yourself or through the press.

Provide a Great End-to-End Experience

The greatest way Apple gets buzz is by making sure the wonderful experiences they provide never end. The Apple experience is not just about the product, but everything about it, such as the experience of buying it in an Apple store. Even the service Apple provides at the Genius Bar is a thrill to customers. Think about that: Even when the product breaks, customers rave! This all generates good buzz for Apple. Sure, they may be Apple, but this can be applied to any startup. Here are some ways to provide a great end-to-end experience that will get people to talk:

- Provide a simple way to register and get started. The less friction the better. When it comes to your product, give before you get.
- Make the first interactions with the product something special that stands out. With iOS5, Apple has a great experience for first-time users that is simple and makes setting up your iPad a fun experience.
- Provide awesome support. Even the most hostile customers will turn into evangelists if you give them a little TLC.

When your startup begins to get attention, an interesting group of individuals being to take notice. Many may be a waste of your time, such as consultants who want to latch on to your success. On the flip side, you may also start to attract the attention of investors who will help accelerate your startup.

10

FROM $1,000 TO $1,000,000

IF YOU PAY attention to the headlines about startups getting millions of dollars of funding from investors, venture capitalists, or partnerships, you might think the fund-raising process happens overnight. It all sounds so easy: Some entrepreneur with a thousand dollars in his pocket creates a great PowerPoint investor presentation, secures a few meetings with important people, and bam! A handshake, some signatures, and the deal is done.

The reality is a little trickier. Fund-raising is a process, and although the right pitch might come in handy, in this chapter I'll discuss the practical start-to-finish way to think about fund-raising that will get you the money you want in the end.

THE REAL PURPOSE OF RAISING MONEY AND WHY IT MIGHT NOT MAKE SENSE FOR YOU

More often than not, entrepreneurs raise money at the wrong time and it destroys their startup. This is an understandable mistake, because the press, the outside world, even your peers put a lot of emphasis on raising money.

If you pitch investors too soon, they may get the wrong notion about your business and decide to pass. Although they have the option of coming back to you at a later date, that is highly unlikely. But even if another opportunity does come along later on, they'll always remember you as the one they passed on the first time around. There is no one reason why an investor passes, What matters is whether they pass on you based on a full picture of what your company really does. But on the off chance that a startup is able to raise money at the wrong time, it will certainly have a negative impact on fundraising at a later date.

When Is the Right Time to Fund-raise?

There are seven questions you should ask yourself when deciding if you are ready to fund-raise:

1. **Do you have a technical cofounder?** If you have a technical cofounder or someone who is focused on product, you are far more likely to raise money. Product drives the growth of a company; having a product-driven founder can generate growth.

2. **Do you have a demo?** If you have a working demo, then you are much more likely to raise money since you can show an investor what your company does. Onswipe was able to fund-raise because we could show investors firsthand exactly what we do. Show, don't tell.

3. **Do you have any customers?** Companies with customers are more likely to raise venture capital than those with-

out. If you don't have customers yet, you should make this a priority, as it shows proof of traction in the market. It's not about the amount of traction, but the proof it shows in your model.

4. **Are you ready to bring more people on board?** You need to be ready to manage other people and expand your team. If you are not ready for this, then you are not ready to raise venture capital. Venture capital lets you do one thing in the beginning: Hire more manpower.

5. **Have you rid yourself of other obligations?** If you are not 100 percent committed to your startup you should hold off on raising money. Many entrepreneurs try to fund-raise while still at their current job. Though it's good to begin a startup before you quit your job, it takes a whole lot more time and effort to raise money.

6. **Is your business large enough?** Most companies are not large enough to be backed by venture capital. To raise venture capital, companies should be in multibillion-dollar markets or have the potential to make revenues of more than one hundred million dollars a year.

7. **Are you able to devote the majority of your time to fund-raising?** Fund-raising is a time-consuming process that will completely slow down all other fast-moving aspects of your company. Be prepared to put business development, product development, and any marketing you may be doing on hold, or at least slow them down for a while. Put together a strategy for keeping operations going while fund-raising. I suggest spending 50 percent of your time on fund-raising and 50 percent on continued op-

erations and product development. One founder should still be moving product development forward.

Making Sure You're Ready to Be a Venture-Backed Founder

Everything changes once you raise money for your company. Your life will be transformed and you and your startup will be on a collision course either with failure or greatness. Most important, being a venture-backed founder means that you will have a great deal of responsibility going forward. That responsibility comes in three forms: responsibility to your employees, responsibility to your customers, and responsibility to your investors.

Just before you raise money, odds are that you are a team of two to three founders. If your startup doesn't turn out well, you'll end up getting a job somewhere or moving on to another idea if you are adventurous. As a venture-backed founder, you have raised money primarily to hire the smartest possible individuals. Their livelihood is now in your hands. Make sure that you are ready as a founder to handle the burden of having many other individuals depending on you. Venture-backed founders need to be entirely selfless.

In the beginning you may have had a small number of customers to prove the viability of your startup over time. If your company disappeared, your customers would certainly have been impacted, but life would have rolled on. Odds are the feature set that you could have deployed would not have been supercrucial to their businesses. As a venture-backed founder, your goal is to grow your product and have explosive growth in the number of your customers. Be ready to take on another burden—many companies will now be relying on your product for some very important function in their business. If you screw up, you screw them up.

Lastly, you have a responsibility to the investors who gave you money. If they are angel investors, the money came from their very own pockets. It's money they earned by going through the very sweat and tears you are currently going through. If your investors are venture investors, they put their reputations and jobs on the line by trusting their limited partners' (that is, your investors' investors) money. Venture capitalists run a business too and they expect to make their money back, often tenfold or more. You now have a responsibility to make them successful.

Know How and Where to Put Your Capital to Work

You need to be able to show your potential investors that you know what you are going to do with the money. If you're hiring people, who are you hiring and why? If you are going to be spending it on equipment, why will the equipment cost so much? You do not need to know exact dollar amounts, but you do need to have a plan for where the money will be spent.

You Probably Need More Than You Think

Investors usually have funds in the hundreds of millions of dollars. Asking for a million dollars instead of half a million won't make a dent in their bank accounts. Although this is your first financing round, you need to think about the long-term game. If you don't raise enough money, you may end up running out of cash too early. Investors only fund a small handful of companies a year. If they believe in your team and your concept, they will want you to execute on the vision properly instead of running out of cash in six months.

On the flip side, it's hard to come back to your investors asking for more after you have already pitched that you're looking for half that amount. A good investor who believes in your vision will insist that you raise more. If you happen to find an investor who suggests this, try to get them in the round. Their thinking is less about themselves and more about your startup succeeding.

HOW TO MEET INVESTORS

The battle for fund-raising is often won long before a single pitch is delivered. Meeting the right investors at the right time is crucial to raising money for your startup successfully. You also need to keep an eye out for those who may not have your best intentions at heart or have weak connections to potential investors. Most important, never, ever pay to pitch an investor or get an introduction.

Find a Champion

Consider the champion for your company a spark who will set off a chain reaction through his introductions. He should be well connected, willing to contribute capital himself, and have your best interests at heart. This person is usually a close connection you meet through the technology community and has already been successful. If you do not have any clout and are a complete outsider, I would spend time getting to know smart, successful entrepreneurs by asking for their advice. It's often hard to get their attention, so this will take a good bit of resilience. Consider your champion the first person to help to get your round started. When the fund-raising process is complete, their introductions should have been where everything else began.

Narrow Down Your List to Those Who Are in Your Sector

Don't try to raise money from every investor under the sun who is willing to listen to you. Fund-raising is a time-consuming game that requires talking to a large number of investors. Do not waste your time—or anyone else's—trying to get a meeting with the wrong person. Narrow down the venture funds and angels on your list that fit some or all of the following criteria:

They invest in and understand your sector. I'm not talking just life sciences or technology. I'm referring to the specific portion of the broader industry you are in. For tech it might be media, data plays, or mobile gaming, for instance.

They are willing to invest in your location and often do so. Investors will often spend time between Boston, New York, and California, but often prefer investing in ventures that don't require a lot of travel. It's much easier for an investor in California to drive forty-five minutes from San Francisco to Palo Alto than it is to take a six-hour flight to Boston. Find investors who live in your area.

They don't already invest in your competitors. Good investors, specifically venture funds, will not want to fund competitive products. Meeting with investors who already fund the competition is not only a waste of your time, but it might also allow them to get information that could be used against you.

Start Leveraging Your Personal Brand Through Writing

Every investor is going to Google you before they take their first meeting with you, let alone give you a boatload of money. When they do, one of the first results they should see is a link to your personal site, which should feature frequently updated writing on your industry. Writing smart things gives investors insight into how you think and communicate as an entrepreneur. If it were not for writing, I would not be where I am today.

Get Portfolio Founders to Make Warm Introductions

Most investors will trust the judgment of their portfolio founders when it comes to future deal flow. A portfolio founder is the founder of another company the investor has previously invested in. Not only are the founders of their portfolio companies smart, they are also in the trenches and know what is happening in the industry. Founders often talk to other smart founders to understand where the industry is going. If you can prove yourself as a smart individual in a smart space with a great product, other portfolio CEOs will introduce you to their investors. This also requires taking time to build relationships with portfolio founders. It can't happen overnight or be forced upon a founder you are asking for an introduction.

Stay Under the Radar

Many would say that talking about your fund-raising during the process is a great way to create hype, but the opposite is true. Being quiet about fund-raising will ensure that you are not analyzed by other individuals if closing the round takes more time than you would like. All investors talk to each other, and by staying under the radar you make sure the conversation stays among those who are a part of the close-knit circle of early investors. The funding announcement will be more exciting and newsworthy when people don't know it's coming.

Go After a Specific Partner at the Fund

Of course it's important to pick the right fund as a target, but you should also pay attention to the specific partner you are talking to. Even at well-known funds, some partners will stand out above the rest and others might not be a good fit for your company. Once you've narrowed down a fund, look at the partners who represent companies that are similar to yours and try to get introduced. Note that there is a difference between "similar" and "competitive." Competitors are companies that compete head on with yours. Similar companies are those in a space a lot like yours, and the expertise learned from one can be transferred to another. When you finally meet this partner, play to her experiences before she became a venture capitalist and to the successes of her portfolio companies. If you focus on language she understands, you will be able to have a much more meaningful conversation and connect with her on a deeper level.

Build Momentum from the Lead

Once your lead investor is in the round, utilize that commitment to get others on board. You have nothing to lose, as the money is already on its way and your lead investor will want to add smart investors to the round. Consider your investors almost like another cofounder who will be on your side while pitching. If you are really lucky, your lead investor will even come with you to the pitch meetings to back you up.

HOW TO PITCH INVESTORS WITHOUT MAKING THEM FALL ASLEEP

Everything you know about pitching investors is wrong. It's not about a boring pitch deck or speaking down to the investor. Investors see hundreds of companies a year and they want to be excited. They don't walk into meetings wanting to say no; they walk into meetings hoping to find an awesome, exciting, and motivating startup. Here's how that startup can be you.

Business Plans Are Dead

Common wisdom holds that you need to have a business plan that shows investors your plan to grow your company over the next five years. But the problem with making long-term projections like that is that events never turn out the way you expect. Things always change, and your business plan will eventually become irrelevant no matter how much time you put into it today.

The good news is that if you ask any serious angel investor or VC they'll tell you that a business plan is a waste of time. They want to know that you have a strong product and customer acquisition strategy and that you are prepared to adapt to changing times. Instead of writing a business plan, it's best to have the following pieces of information crystal clear for the next three to six months (anything beyond that is too open to change in the long run):

1. A clear product strategy that defines what you are building, how you will build it, and why your product is compelling.

2. A clear way to acquire customers and the associated channels.

3. All the potential revenue models that may end up being utilized by the company.

D.R.E.A.M.—Demos Rule Everything Around Me

Humans are visual creatures, and investors, though often made to seem different, are humans too. Nothing will sell an investor more than a slick demo that demonstrates your domain expertise and the way you think about delivering a great product. Don't worry if the product is not perfectly polished. Go for the wow factor and blow an investor out of the water.

Many investors talk to companies first and foremost as users of their products. One of our leading investors was actually our product's first customer. By having a working demo you have the following advantages when talking to an investor:

1. They will be able to understand exactly what you are building. Telling is one thing, but showing offers a whole other level of understanding.

2. If an investor likes the product, they can evangelize it to their vast network for quick social proof and due diligence.

3. If the VC has a product or engineering background, they can easily tell if you are the real deal. It's really difficult to explain things to a VC and have them believe that you can get the job done. If you show some simple proof of concept, they are able to get over that hump.

You will learn more about this in the following section, but make sure to build anticipation for the demo. Jump into it fast enough, but build suspense. Have the investors on the edge of their seats to see what is about to happen.

Tell a Story First

Investors listen to hundreds upon hundreds of pitches per year. After a while, most of them seem exactly the same and offer nothing more than a standard pitch deck showcasing the features of a product or service and explaining why it's going to change the world. But when you're on the other side of things—creating the pitch—it's easy to forget that despite how new, different, or revolutionary your product may actually be, potential investors don't know that yet. If you try to sell yourself the same way everyone else does, you'll be drowned out by all the other noise.

That's why you need a story. As I said, investors are people too. They respond to and are intrigued by the same things as the rest of us. So think about it. If you were them, would you rather have someone pitch to you for thirty minutes or have them tell you a great, unique story that sticks with you? I think I can guess your answer.

Although every startup story is different, there are a few components central to each one:

How the founders met. First, you have to tell the story of how you and your partner (if you have one) met. Investors invest in people first, and they want to make sure before they decide to back your company that the people who run it are smart, engaging and, most important, work well with one another. If investors can see that a founding team has a strong rapport they will be more likely to invest in your company.

Idea genesis. You have to explain how you came up with your idea. Investors want to know that you're inspired and passionate about your product or service, and nothing can demonstrate this more than the story of its genesis. The best startups are the ones that arose from a founder's personal need or desire. If investors see that, they will trust that you are committed to your idea and will be more likely to jump on board.

What you have done. Next give investors an idea of what you have accomplished on a small, limited budget with a small, limited team. If you have good customer growth or a huge business development deal make that clear. Let this early traction show why you decided to take the company to the next level.

The big vision. Of course, where you've been doesn't necessarily determine where you'll go, and in order for investors to get a sense of your company's future you'll need to explain your vision. Big visions don't come overnight The progression from small startup to large, scalable startup takes a lot of intense strategic thinking. Once you explain what the big vision is, you'll need to explain how you are going to get there. It should be tied directly into why you are raising money in the first place.

After you've shared your story, if you've done a good job the investors should be itching for a demo of what you've built. Be sure you have mentioned the demo along the way as a teaser to build anticipation.

Pitch Decks Are Really "Clarification Decks"

I've spent a lot of time dismissing the need for a typical investor presentation, but you should prepare pitch decks that summarize your presentation and that can be distributed as PDFs after (or before) the meeting. Although you shouldn't make them part of your presentation, they can clarify the deeper questions an investor may have when he sits down with you for a one-on-one meeting. Pitch decks challenge an investor's assumptions for or against your startup. What will really sell your startup is the face-to-face conversation.

Play to the Partner's Previous Experience and Domain Expertise

I mentioned this when talking about who to target at a venture fund and why. It's really important to understand the specific partner you are going after. Find out everything you can about his investment thesis, what he likes, and his strategic decisions behind past investments. Toward the end of the first meeting ask him why he invested in certain companies and what made him continue to invest in them. If you can find out what attracted this partner to those investments, parlay some of that logic into your own pitch. You'll be way ahead of the game.

The Partners' Meeting

The partners' meeting is the last step in pitching to a firm. It will ultimately move them toward a yes or a no. Every firm varies in how they approach the partners' meeting. Below are some strategic points to keep in mind when making the partners' meeting pitch:

Get inside information from your sponsoring partner. Find out from your sponsoring partner which partners have significant interest and which ones will be difficult to deal with or have no domain expertise. If you are pitching a consumer Internet product, the enterprise services partner may have objections that do not make sense. Find out all this ahead of time.

Have your sponsoring partner keep the conversation on track. Look to your sponsoring partner as a sort of referee. She brought you in for a reason and wants to see the deal get done. She will be able to keep the conversation on track and make sure the key selling points that brought you in get across to the rest of the partnership.

Pick your battles wisely. Questions that aren't too relevant to your business or crucial to your success may be raised by the other partners in the fund. Other questions that are absolutely critical to your success may come up. Focus on the questions that are most important to you. There isn't enough time to go into every single detail.

Make sure you address everyone. It's really easy to find one partner more engaging than others. Make sure that every single member of the fund gets enough of your attention and answer all questions in the order they are received. It's a rapid-fire environment and you're not being rude just because you want to keep questions organized.

HOW A ROUND CLOSES AND HOW YOU CAN SPEED IT UP

The entrepreneurial community almost never talks about closing your funding round. It's boring, tedious, painful, and the exact opposite of the thrill entrepreneurs are used to. It is rare that funding rounds fall apart after a term sheet is signed, but it's possible. The most important thing is to close a round fast so you can get back to building your business with a good amount of capital in the bank.

The Term Sheet Is Just the First Step

Most entrepreneurs think that receiving a term sheet means the deal is done and they can expect a check the next day. Unfortunately that's not the case. The term sheet is not a legally binding document except in that it stipulates that you can't shop the deal around for 30 days. Raising money takes time and you should be prepared to go from term sheet to money in the bank in 90 to 180 days, depending on how far along your company is. This is something to keep in mind as you plan your finances for the coming months.

When to Have Your VC Firm Step In

Lawyers nitpick at things—not because they are trying to sabotage deals, but because it is their job. Things they might haggle over include whether the VC can fire you or how long you have to stay at the company to earn your stock. Things that often seem not to be a big deal get torn apart and looked at in the due diligence process. The best way around this nuisance is to have the partner at your VC firm step in. Have a discussion with them about the issue, come to a conclusion, and then have them circle back with their counsel. The VC wants the deal done too and will move to make it happen fast as long as you are being reasonable. Only turn to your VC on serious matters (such as the rights that protect you as a founder) or if you think the process will be slowed down otherwise.

Keeping Your Mouth Shut

When you have a term sheet for more money than you may ever have seen in your life, you will want to jump up and down and tell everyone you know. But don't let yourself get carried away and definitely don't announce the deal just yet. The press will pick up on it and they will publish any secret details they can. That won't necessarily kill the deal, but it could get an investor worried enough to pull the funding offer. It is not worth taking that chance. Get back to work and keep your mouth shut throughout the entire process. You want to introduce as few new variables into the process as possible.

Surviving the Holidays

Almost everyone will tell you that the holidays are a horrible time to raise a round of financing and close it. I actually believe the opposite is true if you are able to move fast enough and be organized. Everyone else is clamoring to get deals done during peak times, leaving little room for you. Though the holidays may be a slow time, there are fewer interruptions from other startups and companies, and if an investor loves a deal they will push to get it closed. Lawyers get paid exorbitant fees, and though they may charge you a little bit more to work during this season they will get the deal done.

Rounding Up All Members of the Round

Make sure you have all the necessary information from those investing in your company when you are about to close the round. This might include things like agreements between founders and intellectual property agreements. The best way to get things done is to introduce your lawyer to your investor; the lawyer will then get the signed documents from the investor independently. The other key thing your law firm will do is send the information needed for money to be wired. Asking for money might feel weird to a newly minted entrepreneur, but in this case the lawyer casually takes care of it by sending along a wire transfer sheet.

HOW WE RAISED $1,000,000 FOR ONSWIPE IN UNDER FORTY DAYS

This is the unfiltered and true story of how we raised one million dollars for Onswipe. Don't be surprised if your experience is much different, but it's always good to understand how the process can play out.

The Precursor: Introductions and Failed Pitches

Andres and I spent two weeks kicking off our fund-raising primarily on the West Coast in the fall of 2010, two weeks after our launch. The meetings went well, but for the most part we were getting rejected. We had asked ourselves the seven questions outlined earlier in the chapter, which made us believe it was time to fund-raise, and decided to go after five hundred thousand dollars. We had a few angel commitments totaling close to seventy-five thousand dollars, but nothing outstanding. We were sleeping on floors, spending our personal money, traveling all over, and we were exhausted. We were lucky, though, that we were able to get a large number of introductions from a champion who believed in us. Our champion was Roy Rodenstein, a serial entrepreneur who had successfully sold his company to AOL. He was kind and willing to introduce us to every VC he knew as he believed in us and wanted us to succeed. Eventually we got a first meeting with the VC firm that would lead our round. Our earlier failed pitches had taught us to think bigger and focus on the opportunities our product presented around advertising. Many viewed us only as a WordPress plugin. Then, on December 2, 2010, we secured a meeting that would change our lives.

First Meeting: December 2, 2010, 2:00 P.M.

Our first meeting with Spark Capital took place at 2:00 P.M. in Boston and was scheduled for an hour. Spark Capital has backed the likes of Tumblr, Twitter, and Foursquare. I told the story of our vision while delivering an awesome demo and didn't use a slide deck at all . I was the only person present at the meeting as Andres was on his way back to the West Coast. I knew the meeting was going well when Alex Finkelstein, a partner who is now our lead investor and a board member, brought Andrew Parker, another member of the firm, into the meeting. We all saw eye-to-eye on the product and the vision. Something just clicked.

Approximately five minutes after the meeting ended my phone rang and Alex asked if I could come back with Andres the following Tuesday for a partners' meeting. He said he wouldn't ask this if he didn't really like us and the company. I already had plans to be in California then, but I said we'd make it. I left Andres a message with the awesome news while he was on a plane to San Francisco, expecting to be there until Christmas. We changed our plans and booked a flight back east for that Sunday.

Partners' Meeting: December 7, 2010, 10:30 A.M.

We had our partners' meeting on the morning of December 7, 2010, and although we had a decent idea of what to expect, we still weren't sure what would happen. As I've said, at a partners' meeting you deal with every partner in the firm, including those who may not be in your sector. You have to be able to keep the conversation on course and answer questions from everybody. We brought in our PowerPoint deck, even though Alex had suggested that a conversation would work better. At the end of the day, we set up the PowerPoint presentation but never used it because we ended up focusing on our demo and explaining the big vision. We realized at the meeting that Spark Capital would be the right firm for Onswipe in the long run. They asked questions that indicated they understood we were an advertising and media company, not a software company. A software company would charge a one-time fee for the use of the product, whereas an advertising play would compete on audience size. The meeting felt like one large product brainstorm. The people at Spark clearly understood how we would build the business for the long haul. The meeting stayed on track and we felt good about it, but it was hard to judge what would happen next. Would they say no? Would they think about it more? Would they say yes?

Term Sheet Offer: December 7, 2010, 12:30 P.M.

At around 12:30 P.M. that day my life and my cofounder's life forever changed. Andres and I were grabbing lunch at the Wendy's on Boylston Street when the familiar phone number from Spark Capital showed up on my caller ID. I took the call and it was Alex. He told us he would like to fund Onswipe, but not for five hundred thousand dollars. He wanted to give us a million. I mouthed to Andres, "They want to fund us! They want to give us one million fucking dollars!" Alex and I quickly talked about deal terms and who else we would like in the syndicate (the group of investors that participates in a funding round). The term sheet would be to us in the next twenty-four hours.

Term Sheet Signed: December 10, 2010, 11:00 A.M.

Soon after our meeting with Spark, we had to head down to New York City to meet with the heads of TechStars, David Tisch and David Cohen. We had received the first revision of the term sheet on December 8, had a few comments from our lawyers, and signed the final term sheet on December 10 after coming back from New York the night before. The lawyers were off to the races putting together the actual closing documents and we were about to go fill out our syndicate.

We Close Second Largest Investor: December 14, 2010

Though Spark had committed to putting in the full one million dollars, we had to choose between letting them take only half a million and bringing in other investors to join the round. We had an existing relationship with Betaworks, a medium-sized young company that invests in and starts new companies such as bitly and TweetDeck, because their CEO was our first customer. Alex, our lead investor at Spark, was in New York that day and already planned to be at Betaworks. We decided we should all get together for a meeting: team Onswipe, Alex, and the Betaworks founders. In one of the most epic moments of entrepreneurship ever, Alex perfectly pitched Onswipe for two minutes to the Betaworks guys. Soon after, Andy Weissman, the COO of Betaworks, looked at John Borthwick, the CEO, and asked. "Do you want to invest?" John responded, "Yup, let's do it." That was it. Within forty-five minutes, with our VC's help, we closed Betaworks, the leading early stage investment vehicle in New York.

Lawyers Get Started on Closing Docs

The holidays were rolling around and our lawyers had started preparing the closing documents. Along with the documents, we needed to send over a vast wealth of information as part of the due diligence process. Luckily, we had our documents and records well organized from the beginning. I had officially become not only the CEO of Onswipe but also the general counsel, it seemed. The hustle was well worth it as we were able to get the round closed fast and money in the bank easily.

All Angels Onboard: December 27, 2010

Throughout the process we grew the syndicate to a total of eight participants ranging from individual investors to Spark, a large venture fund. Once Spark was in the rest of the process took care of itself. Though we added several participants, each of them had a specific reason for being in the round, namely their domain expertise and potential value. The hardest part was saying no to investors, especially those who supported and believed in what we were doing. We could have raised way more money but we did not want to sell more of the company so we had to turn away investors. Don't add investors to the round just to add them. Make sure each person brings true value.

Round Closed and Money in the Bank: January 4, 2011

Early in the morning of January 3, 2010, I e-mailed our lawyers asking if all the final documents were taken care of. I received a response indicating that everything was closed and the wire for the funds had been initiated. I soon went to check our bank account and found more money in one place than I had ever seen before. I tweeted out a few minutes later: "Boom. Let's do this."

Funding Announcement: January 12, 2011, 10:00 P.M.

According to SEC rules, we had fifteen days from closing before the deal became public record. We decided on January

13, 2011, as the day we would announce our big news to the world. A fork was thrown into the works as *TechCrunch*, which would be breaking the story, decided they wanted to run it the night before. They knew we were changing our branding to coincide with our investment and did not want the story about our investment to leak early. We scrambled to tie up some loose ends and were soon ready for the announcement. At 10:00 P.M. on the dot, we announced we had raised "Like, a Million Dollars."

We Add the Best West Coast Investors: January 17, 2011

In our legal documents, there was a stipulation providing for a sixty-day period during which we could add more investors to the round. We talked with our current lineup and realized we had zero West Coast representation. We had the best investors in Boston and New York, but needed to get the best from the West. In a matter of forty-eight hours, without any face-to-face meetings, we were able to add SV Angel and Morado Ventures. SV Angel is the fund that Ron Conway, the so-called "Godfather of Silicon Valley," helps run. Ron is an investor in every major Internet phenomenon including Google, Twitter, Facebook, and others. Morado Ventures gave us access to the network of early Yahoo! employees and those who had helped build the company from the ground up. We now had the entire country covered and were ready to take over the world.

Final Thought: Funding Is *Not* the Endgame

Though a large achievement for a startup, funding is just one achievement of many. A long road lies ahead that will consume your life for the next five to ten years. It will be a roller coaster of ups and downs that will test your endurance. In reality, being a funded startup means the odds are against you. Most venture-backed startups end up failing, which is why the venture business is a high-risk, high-reward class. Your goal once you're funded is to do one thing: Stay alive.

11

HOW NOT TO DIE

A STARTUP IS a marathon, not a sprint. When you launch your startup, the excitement and adrenaline can be enough to keep you going. But as you start to settle in, the thrill will taper off into long hours, frustration, and a prevailing worry about "What if I fail?!" Quitting may seem like it would be a relief when you feel like you're staring into the abyss on a daily basis and might as well be eating glass for all the joy you're getting out of the process. But it's the ability to conquer the difficult days that separates great companies from dead ones. Luckily, there are a few steps you can take that will make this feel a little more doable.

STAY SANE AND DON'T BURN OUT

This will be the hardest "job" you have ever had and most likely ever will (until you launch your next startup, that is). Building a company is like running a marathon that lasts for years and only gets more competitive as you become more successful. Here are some of my favorite things to do to stay sane and keep calm.

Make Friends Outside Business

It's great to have friends inside the entrepreneurial community as they can understand the pains you go through and give you advice on how to move forward, but hanging out with people as intense as you are can also be overwhelming. The easiest way for me to relax is to hang out with people I grew up with or those I met outside the technology industry. Entrepreneurs are competitive, and being around others who are doing what you're doing will make you feel like you need to talk about your product or compare your startup with others. Sometimes you just need to take a break, and there is nothing better for this than hanging out with a group of friends who have nothing to do with your work.

Take Three Days Off Every Six Months

Three days off every six months sounds like what you might allow an indentured servant, but it is more time than you think. When you're working in a fast-paced industry, scrambling to stay alive, it can be difficult to justify taking any time off, but it is helpful to disconnect for a few days every so often. Figuring out when to do so requires planning. You should only do it when you're between major releases, but if you don't figure it out in advance you'll never find time to breathe. Make sure your company will be able to survive without you for a few days because if it isn't you will do nothing but worry. Take a step back, breathe, and realize that nothing will crumble in three days.

Brainstorm New Product Innovations

When you are working on the same product cycle for too long, you often forget what it's like to come up with something new and innovative. If you ever feel like you are at this point, try to come up with new ideas heavily related to your startup. They may not be ideas you can execute for a long time or until you have a significant amount of capital, but they can inspire new creativity in day-to-day activities.

Find a Microhobby

Hobbies can be expensive and time consuming, but microhobbies do not need to cost a ton and can be done at your leisure. My original microhobby was blogging, and this is what ultimately led me to come up with the idea for Onswipe. The best kinds of microhobbies are not passive, like watching TV, but ones that let you express yourself or physically let loose. My other microhobby is running and working out. I have run 5K every day for over two years straight as a way to keep my dedication up, but also to clear my mind for a little while each day.

THE HARSH REALITIES OF BEING AN ENTREPRENEUR

Entrepreneurs can reap a ton of rewards, but to get them they need to overcome a ton of challenges. Many of these are common enough that pretty much every entrepreneur goes through them, but with a little effort and support they're not so difficult to overcome. My hope is that when you encounter these difficulties you will think back on this book and say, "Wow, I remember hearing about this. Now I'm actually going through it." Don't worry. Smile and remember that it's going to be okay.

You Will Not Make Much Money for a While

Make no mistake about it, you will be borderline broke for close to a year. Entrepreneurship is about making money, but for a good while you will have to give up a lot of material possessions that you are used to. Prepare to eat (cheap) pizza, forgo things you love, and not be able to go out as often as you used to. When you finally do have money, you will certainly make below market rate. There is no overnight success and money won't fall into your lap. You need to be prepared for making close to nothing. Although larger cities like New York and San Francisco (where most of the action in the tech sector happens) are more costly, they have a large array of activities to keep you busy. If you can find a way to bootstrap yourself in one of these cities, you'll benefit from the excitement of the concrete jungle.

Everything Takes Twice as Long . . . if It Even Happens at All

No matter how likely it seems that a deal will go through, the closing process will always take longer than you think it will. Remember that nothing is closed until it is closed, and even then someone can come along to screw you over. Entrepreneurship requires a lot of patience, and things only become more complicated and time-consuming as the deals get bigger. Even when you're playing a waiting game, you need to move the ball forward continually in terms of gaining customers and growing the product. Just like football, entrepreneurship is a game of inches.

Success Does Not Happen Overnight and It Doesn't Always Last Forever

Reading about successful startups in the media can make you feel as if everything can and will happen overnight. But these stories never reveal what happened in between the beginning and the end. Remember that a press article is just a snapshot in time: If the story you're reading is about a success, it will never fully highlight the difficulties encountered over time, and if the story is about a failure, it will never fully highlight the successes along the way. A famous article in *BusinessWeek* in 2006 highlighted Digg's CEO, Kevin Rose, as the sixty-million-dollar kid running a two-hundred-million-dollar company. But what the article didn't say was that Digg took awhile to build into a success and had a lot of struggles along the way. Never look at a snapshot; look at the full picture. Success can turn into failure much faster than failure can turn to success. You should always be just as hungry and willing to succeed as when you were a complete nobody.

No One Will Quite Understand What You Do

No matter how great your idea is, your family, your friends, and just about any stranger on the street will think you are crazy if you tell them what you're doing. Until you have made it, they will never understand what you do or what drives you to do it. Most will try to convince you to get a "normal job" or will have an uninformed opinion about why your idea will never work. Holidays will be rough as everyone will want to know what you have been up to. Stay calm, stay confident, and do not let it faze you. Don't let the questions and lack of understanding get to you. If you don't feel like talking with someone about what you do, be as vague as possible and tell him you work in the "software industry" or at an "Internet media company."

There Is No Silver Bullet

All entrepreneurs have a feature epiphany that they think will make the company go from mediocrity to greatness, a moment when they think they've found the silver bullet that will make everything work and launch them to startup stardom. But success cannot be measured with one major victory; it's the sum of all the small victories that happen along the way.

The First Version of Your Product Will Suck

If you are not embarrassed by the first version of your product then either you waited too long to launch it or you have an insanely large ego. You need to ship something fast and should not be concerned with it being on par with a competitor or another company that you look up to. Go take a look at the first versions of Google's home page, Facebook's site, or the first personal computer. They were all pretty crappy in retrospect, but they did one thing and one thing well. I remember our first version of PadPressed. It was an abomination, but it was the first thing of its kind. People understood that it was early and that we were going into uncharted territory.

Customers Will Be Assholes

Unless you are a saint, you have acted like an asshole as a customer—and so has everyone else. In the world of Twitter and social media, everyone feels like they're the center of attention just because they have been given a platform from which to voice their thoughts. You should certainly treat customers well, but sometimes they will ask too much of you. Do not let those with unreasonable demands or harsh words get you down. Instead, "kill them with kindness" and rise above it.

Your Title Is Worthless

So many entrepreneurs love to "play CEO." They think they are hot shit because they have created a company from scratch and assumed the CEO title. If you're one of these people, check yourself fast, because you're broke, underfunded, and still have a long way to go. The *real* CEO is a great leader who builds a great business with great people. Until you've done this, refer to yourself as cofounder, not as CEO.

You Can't Do It All by Yourself

I said this in Chapter Five, but it's worth reiterating. When you are the cofounder of a startup, you will develop a Superman complex. You will start to think you can do everything yourself, even if it's something your cofounder or a freelancer can do equally well or even better. The best leaders know how to delegate, and if you don't know how to delegate you're going to die. Realize that building a business is a team sport, check your ego at the door, and ask for help when you need it. There is no shame in that.

Building a Team Is Hard

It is incredibly difficult to build a great team. Entrepreneurs often spend 50 percent of their time building out their team in the form of advisers, contractors, employees, and investors. The best companies succeed by filling their staffs with the best people possible. This is tough when you are undercapitalized, because very few people will want to join you. If you are the CEO, your biggest advantage is your vision, so you need to sell the dream. Convince those you want to hire that they can be part of something big and make sure they understand the goal.

There Are Things You Cannot Control

Most entrepreneurs will move mountains to make the impossible become possible, but that doesn't mean you can do everything. There are some things that are simply out of your control. Someone may lose her job, macroeconomic circumstances might affect your business, or disaster may strike. There is no way to get around these scenarios. You need to take a deep breath and figure out how to deal with whatever. Recognize that there are situations you cannot control and don't blame yourself.

A FAREWELL

THE END OF this book is just the beginning. Maybe you read each chapter as you went along with the process, but odds are that you're just now ready to begin a great journey. Things will get tough, and you may fail, but the one thing you can be sure of is that you will have the time of your life. I hope you will come back to this book as a point of reference at pivotal moments such as your first fund-raise or making your first big hire. I can't respond to everyone, but if you want to share your progress or thoughts about the journey, feel free to e-mail me at j@jasonlbaptiste.com.

And remember: Dream big. Build bigger.

_____

A YEAR IN THE LIFE OF
A STARTUP

THE BLOW-BY-BLOW ACCOUNT OF
ONSWIPE'S FIRST YEAR

_____

The year after starting Onswipe was a wild ride. In the beginning, I was in the same exact shoes you are in right now with nothing but an idea and the belief that something big could come of it. We had absolutely no money and were walking eleven miles a day around San Francisco looking for funding, but within six months we had raised two rounds of venture capital for a total of six million dollars. Inside of one year Andres and I were able to grow from two people all the way up to fifteen employees. This is the story of how we did it. I hope it serves as guidance and inspiration for you on your journey.

June 3, 2010: The Idea

Onswipe came about as a solution to a simple problem that I and Andres Barreto, wanted to solve. We were both blogging

_____

heavily at the time; I was gaining popularity at jasonlbaptiste .com and Andres was growing pulsosocial.com into a very popular blog for Latin American entrepreneurs. In June 2010, Andres went to speak in Colombia for a weekend while I stayed home trying to make my blog more readable on the iPad. The world of the touch-enabled Web is way different from point-and-click, and everything built in the past wasn't meant for touch interactions and swipe gestures.

When Andres returned after that weekend, I found out he'd been working on the same problem for his blog. We knew the iPad was becoming an important device, and we wanted to figure out a way for our readers to enjoy our content on this new device. We had the option of developing an app, but we wanted to provide the experience to our existing audience, which was visiting and reading our writing on a daily basis. Apps did not make sense to us because our audience already came directly to our blog, and we didn't see the point in directing them to another destination. We decided to create a simple WordPress plugin. Even if no one else used our product, we would still have figured out how to render our content better. We would also have learned a lot about HTML5 and touch interfaces, which would be a valuable skill to have. We couldn't really see any downside, and on the upside, we realized we might be able to make some money in addition to the consulting we were both doing.

June 21 to July 26, 2010: The First Build

Onswipe started out as a WordPress plugin called PadPressed. The first thing we did was to spec out exactly how the product would work and which user interface we wanted to utilize.

After we finished the spec, we decided to send it around to some of our friends in the WordPress community to get their input on the concept. We got some great feedback and decided that it made sense to move forward with the project since we knew that people other than ourselves would want to use it. We also gathered valuable feedback about what features should be included. At this point, we knew we were onto something, and it was off to the races!

At the time, we were working closely with a designer named Armando Sosa on our earlier project, Cloudomatic. Cloudomatic was based on WordPress, so we knew Armando would have a good idea about how to make a WordPress plugin work. But there were a few major roadblocks:

1. Armando was in Mexico and iPads were not available in Mexico yet.
2. iPads were sold out for at least another forty days in the United States, so there was no way we could ship one to him.
3. No one had ever built anything like this before.

In order to attack the first two problems, we decided to record videos of what was happening on the iPad and send them to Armando. This was actually a great way to get feedback as he could see exactly what was wrong. We talked to him on Skype so we could give him feedback in real time while showing him what was happening on the iPad. Our disadvantage actually became an advantage.

July 27, 2010: Our First Launch

We had our first launch on July 27, 2010, after a little over a month of development. We had tested the product thoroughly, put together the Web site copy, and had everything ready to go for a press outreach. One of the most profound moments in our company's history that I remember was a phone call I had with Andres the night before we launched. "Wouldn't it be funny," I said to him, "if this thing takes off and we end up dedicating the next decade to it?" After using the pitch highlighted in Chapter Nine, we received a massive amount of attention from the tech industry as well as paying customers. The site was already live, and the launch really occurred once the press gave it attention.

August to October 2010: Second Build

We had a good amount of success with PadPressed. After seeing it gain some traction and learning the basics of the technology, we were not only excited at the prospect of improving the product, but we realized there had to be something more here. We decided to release a stellar new version with great visuals to see how the public would respond. It made sense to us to devote more time to it and "peel away another layer." We focused specifically on one thing: doing the great things native apps could do, but doing them within the browser. We added unseen HTML5 effects when it came to swiping between pages and transitions between articles. This sounds like a simple task, but it was nearly impossible at the time—and still is, because of all the technology required to pull it off.

October 19, 2010: Why Not Ads?

As we continued to develop the product, we decided to go ahead and investigate how we might become a very large business. Andres and I wanted something we could sink our teeth into for the long haul, something without a ceiling on our vision. We realized that charging a small licensing fee of fifty dollars for a WordPress plugin would not make us millionaires, so we asked ourselves a few questions:

1. How big would the tablet market get?

2. What was the best way to get to a large audience?

3. What was the best way to monetize a large audience?

Since we had started the company, we had seen more and more data that showed that the tablet market was going to be bigger than we could ever have imagined. At the time, the iPad had grown more than any other consumer electronics device in history. We knew that the best way to get the largest audience was to give the software to publishers for free and to build up an audience around the idea of "experience," the same way Google built an audience around the idea of "search." We realized we could do big business by bringing the premium of print advertising to the Web, which was now possible for the first time thanks to these devices. Instead of ugly banner ads and text link ads being the dominant form of Internet advertising, our service could become the new standard.

October 22, 2010: Our Second Launch

Now that we had a new version of the product to complement the big vision we had, we were ready to take the company in a new direction. We gave a press exclusive to *TechCrunch* (as we had done with our first launch), who gladly covered the launch after seeing how much the product had progressed. In the week after our second launch we increased our customer base twofold and started to receive inbound interest from investors. This gave us a great gut feeling that we were on to something.

November 9, 2010: California, Here We Come

At this point, Andres and I knew that we were dedicated to taking Onswipe to the next level. We had changed the name once we decided to raise money and make the company into more than just a plugin. I had previously lived in Silicon Valley and Andres also knew it was the place to make something big happen. We pooled our money and agreed we'd give it a go out there in order to have the largest impact possible. Andres arrived first, on November 9, and I joined him a few days later. This was a big move for both of us financially, personally, and mentally (I was in Boston at the time). We decided to split our time between the East Coast and the West Coast. We rented a room in San Francisco for seven hundred dollars a month and would travel back and forth between Boston and San Francisco on the cheap. We'd rotate who would sleep on the floor and who would get the bed, since we only had enough money for one room.

November 10, 2010: Let's Raise Money

We had a huge vision, but we knew that in order to realize it we would need a fair amount of capital. To begin, we decided to tap our network for potential investors. At the time, my network had grown a little bit as a result of my writing. A few days before I headed to San Francisco, I met with Roy Rodenstein, an investor we had serendipitously met through a mutual contact. I told him about our vision and plan to raise money. Roy believed in us and offered to make introductions to other investors. His connections led to us raising our first round of venture capital.

November 21, 2010: Pizza and TechStars

Even though we had decided to settle in Silicon Valley, Andres and I knew the company would eventually have to have a presence in New York. Our main customer base would be advertisers and publishers and New York was the publishing and advertising capital of the world. We had heard that TechStars was accepting applications for its inaugural New York program, but we held off on applying. Then one night, as I was surfing Twitter while waiting for a pizza to be delivered, I saw a tweet from Dave Tisch, head of TechStars NYC, saying that applications were due in a couple of hours. We decided to apply at the last minute, and even though the application almost didn't get submitted because of a poor Internet signal and my pizza delivery arriving, in the end, we were one of the eleven startups accepted—out of six hundred applications.

November 30, 2010: Going with My Gut

Roy had scheduled a meeting with Spark Capital, a great fund behind companies like Twitter, Tumblr, and Boxee. So when I headed back east to collect some things in preparation for my move to New York, I drove to New Jersey to the Spark Capital offices. I was excited about the meeting but wasn't expecting anything too crazy to happen. As you read in Chapter Ten, things went well, we hit it off, and we were asked to fly back the next week for a partners' meeting. I still went to California for a few days in between and Andres and I met with a prestigious firm that wanted us to pitch their partnership the same day. We could not have a partners' meeting with both firms, so we went with our gut and chose Spark.

December 7, 2010: $1,000,000

We flew back to Boston for the partners' meeting in the hope that we could raise about five hundred thousand dollars. We went into the meeting with confidence, knowing that we would be victorious if we did our job right. We ended up not only doing well but raising double the money we expected— one million dollars.

December 10, 2010: Term Sheet Signed

Early the morning after we received the offer from Spark, the firm sent over a formal term sheet that outlined the major deal points the legal paperwork would be based upon. Most entrepreneurs would be giddy with excitement and sign whatever was thrown their way. The term sheet was very favorable to us, but we still took a good seventy-two hours to make sure all the points were satisfactory to both sides. We only changed a few small details that were recommended to us by our lawyer.

December 10, 2010 to January 3, 2011: Paralegal Wannabe

As CEO, I was the go-between for Onswipe and Spark Capital. For the few weeks after we signed the term sheet and the money was wired into our bank account, I played full-on paralegal. Having no legal experience, this was very nerve racking for me, but it was well worth it. I was able to corral both our lawyers and our investors' lawyers to get the deal done during the holidays. This was important because we wanted to hit the ground running at the beginning of the year.

January 4, 2011: That's a Lot of Zeros

On January 4, 2011, I had finally packed up all my belongings and was ready to make the move to New York to run Onswipe and be part of the TechStars inaugural class. In between packing boxes and having a good-bye dinner with friends, which included our future cofounder and CTO, Mark Bao, the seed round officially closed. Suddenly, there was more money in our bank account than I had ever seen in my life. I thought there would be some sort of crazy change in my life, a big sigh of relief, or just *something* different. But when I actually checked our account balance, I simply sent a screenshot to Andres, had a big smile, and got back to work.

January 6, 2011: 325 East Tenth Street

On January 6, I boarded a bus from Boston to New York. Andres and I did not know the city well at all, but we knew we had to get a place to live quickly and without a lot of hassle because we wanted to be able to focus all our time and energy on the company. We were lucky enough to find short-term temporary housing in the East Village, which ended up being the best place to live as a young twenty-something professional. Even though there was a huge amount of pressure on us now, we also took in the adventure of moving to the best city in the world.

January 11, 2011: "Onswipe Raises, Like, a Million Dollars"

We had a fifteen-day window to announce our new funding to the public. So a week after closing the round we decided to do just that. This was a big day for us, as the rest of the world had no idea we had a larger vision or were raising any money at all. No one knew we were in New York either. We also realized that this would put a lot of attention on us and people's perceptions of us might change a tiny bit. We made the announcement on *TechCrunch,* which we felt loyal to since they had written about us for months. They were afraid someone would steal the scoop, so they asked us to make the announcement a day earlier than we'd planned, which we agreed to. *TechCrunch* had been supportive of us from the beginning and they were the industry leader for breaking news, so we wanted it to happen there. It also helped that they had a huge audience.

February 1, 2011: EJ

Late on the night of February 1, Dave Tisch, the managing director of TechStars, sent me an e-mail about a talented engineer who had worked on multitouch interfaces and was looking for a startup to join. EJ had done a ton of research in an area that was key to Onswipe's success, but we wanted to see if it could translate to what we were doing. We decided to have him create a demo using the iPad and multitouch. We gave him a simple HTML file and said: Show us what you can do. What he ended up doing was mind-blowing: a recreation of the iBooks by Apple page curled inside of a Web browser. Before making a decision about EJ, I happened to show his work to the Apple employee who created the iBooks page curl itself. He almost fell out of his seat and said, "How the fuck did you do that?" That was it. We would hire EJ.

February 11, 2011: Mark Bao

Mark Bao, a college student at the time, was a good friend of mine. We had worked in the past on a family sharing app called Genevine. We both had aspirations to do something big. He was the smartest person I knew, so I thought he would be a good addition to Onswipe. Mark wanted to get to know New York better and we wanted to get him involved in what we were building, at least for the short term. After explaining what we wanted to build, we were able to get Mark down from Boston on a good-sized stipend to help us out on the weekends.

April 11, 2011: On to the Next Round

Over the first four months of our existence we were getting a lot of attention and starting to realize we had hit on a real pain point in the market. What we were building was way larger than we ever thought and we had the right formula down. So in the run-up to demo day, the day that TechStars companies raise money, we decided it was time for another round of fund-raising. At the same time, all our investors wanted to see us accelerate and double down on the opportunity. We decided to go after five million dollars, five times more than we already had. The fund-raising process for this round was simpler than the first round, but a different exercise than the seed round.

April 14, 2011: Pink Shirts and Declarations of Bullshit

The big event for any accelerator program like TechStars is demo day, when all the startups show off what they have built and attempt to raise their first round of funding. Onswipe was in a unique position because we had raised our first round, and we already knew we were doing another round and the terms of that deal. The event was swarming with press as well as a ton of influential people in the technology community. We wanted to use the day to create a splash with the press and get a memorable message out there in front of everybody. I took steps to help us stand out by wearing a bright pink shirt, uttering the catch line "APPS ARE BULLSHIT," and letting everyone know we were raising five million dollars in Series Awesome financing. The real term is "Series A," but we changed it

potential. *See* Customers,
  attracting
shared base and partnering,
  125–26
unreasonable, handling, 202
Customers, attracting, 101–21
  by About.com, 111
  affiliate programs, 114–16
  by Amazon, 115–16
  blogging, 101–2
  by business cofounder, 86
  by Dropbox, 113–14
  by Mint, 102
  in-person events, 75, 117–21
  public relations, 103–5
  referral programs, 112–14
  SEO (search engine
    optimization), 109–11
  social sharing, 105–8
  by threewords.me, 107–8
  types of customers, 50
  Web advertising, 116–17
  by WePay, 103–5
  by WordPress, 120–21
  by Zynga, 117

Damage control, 164–66
Data access, revenues from,
  144–45
Delegation, 202–3
Demand, measuring, 56–58
Design of product
  designer, finding, 32
  for MVP, 23, 31–33
Digg, 200
Dodgeball, 19–20
Dogfooding, 88
Domain expertise, finding for
  startup, 16, 83
Dorsey, Jack, 9–10
DoubleClick, 99
Double viral loop, 107–8

Dropbox
  as better versus new service,
    10–11
  freemium model by, 134–35
  media attention to, 157
  open APIs, 128
  referral program of, 113–14

83(b) election, 69
EJ, 215
E-mail address, 37
Employee compensation
  for advisers, 100
  equity versus salary, 77
  freelance rates, 92–93, 95
Employees, 96–98
  freelancers hired as, 96–98
  intellectual rights agreements
    with, 70
  new talent, finding, 82–86, 215
  paying. *See* Employee
    compensation
Entrepreneurs
  burnout, avoiding, 196–98
  challenges for, 198–203
  Internet, influence on, 2
  passion, need for, 16–17, 20–21
  past conception of, 1–3
  See also Starting company
Equity division agreements, 67–68
Experts
  finding for startup, 16, 82–86,
    215
  See also Cofounders; Hiring

Facebook
  advertising model of, 142–43
  on contact page, 47
  Facebook Connect, 13
  initial version, 18, 201
  News Feed uproar, 165–66
  open API of, 129